A place called Hellhole Swamp

LIFE ON A FARM DURING WORLD WAR TWO AND BEYOND

by Sam Lewis

Sam Lewis

11-2014

****

This book is dedicated to my Mom and Dad
Mae and Clayton Lewis

Shown above in 1927
She was 17 and he was 21 years old

****

My Ancestors

This story begins in the mid-thirties in Berkeley County of South Carolina. It is written in memory of my Father Joe Clayton Lewis who was born September 9, 1907 and died on January 11, 1989 (he was 82), and my Mother Mary Mae White Lewis who was born May 5, 1911 and died on July 5, 2002 (she was 95).

My Father's grandfather, James Whiteford Lewis was born in 1850 and migrated from the coastal area of North Carolina around 1870. He met and married Jane A. Fort and had ten children, eight girls and two boys. The oldest, James Edward Lewis was born in 1876 just after the Civil War. He married Ida Dora Shuler (daughter of Lemuel Shuler and Martha Mitchum). They had thirteen children, nine boys and four girls. The oldest son, Joe Clayton Lewis, was born in 1907 and married Mary Mae White on January 17 1928. She was the daughter of Daniel White and Caroline Mills.

My Mother's grandfather, James Brittian White, was born in 1808. He was an immigrant from England of British and Indian decent. He married Mary M. Fort and had seven children, five girls and two boys. The youngest son, Daniel Oscar White, was born in 1862 and married a Mary L. who died in child birth. He later married Caroline Elizabeth Mills, who was not quite fifteen at the time, and had twelve children. The tenth child, born in 1911, was a daughter named Mary Mae White who later married Joe Clayton Lewis on January 17 1928, when she was seventeen years old. By 1934 they had a son and two daughters. They are going to become my Mom and Dad.

Preface

In 1989, I decided to write about my life to preserve the history of where I came from and to share how the circumstances of my birth, how I was raised, things I was taught and the way I was treated growing up, shaped me into the person I became throughout my life. So, I decided to put my thoughts on tape. At that time, my job in upper management with a large southern department store chain had me traveling quite a bit. As I traveled, I would turn on my tape recorder and in the quiet of my car, began to record recollections from my past. In the process of putting these on tape, other things came to me that had been stored away in my mind. Whether it was growing up on a farm during the Depression, being teased and taunted during my teenage years, quitting high school and getting a job, or encountering tragedy and my own depression, the memories kept coming.

I also recognized that for much of my life, there was something missing. At a crucial point, I doubted God's existence and challenged Him to prove He was real. This story is about my life, and the twists and turns that put me where I was destined to be at a particular time. From meager beginnings, to a successful career, and into retirement, I share how my life unfolds to show that He is truly in control.

The process of writing this autobiography took more than just a couple of years. I started recording my thoughts in 1989 and after accumulating a number of tapes of information, gave the recordings to my youngest daughter to type. Time went by and after she had them for a year or more I finally asked her about them. Unfortunately, her two children had pulled the tapes out of the cassettes so everything I had recorded to that point was gone. So, I started over, recording my thoughts again. This continued for a number of years and finally, in 2005, I began to transcribe the tapes myself, sitting at my computer, pecking away with two fingers. I also spent numerous hours collecting and scanning old photos, looking through school yearbooks, and searching the internet to learn about writing an autobiography and how to publish it yourself. Google Earth provided street level views of places I had been and where I had lived which allowed me to use those images to help the reader visualize my story better, and "Create Space" through Amazon provided me the means to self-publish the finished product. In 2014, after nine years of typing, revising, researching, and adding to the book as more memories came to me, my 70,000 word autobiography was finally finished.

I didn't do it on my own though. My wife, as well as my brothers and sisters provided information that helped to flesh out many of my stories, and my oldest daughter spent countless hours editing and putting my individual stories together in a way that provides the reader with what I hope is an interesting journey. As you go with me, remember that amazing things can happen if you "never give up."

My deepest gratitude to my oldest daughter, Sammie Kay Lewis, for her hard work and persistence in pulling me back from the brink with all the changes I kept making. She has done a wonderful job in editing this document so you the reader can enjoy the journey.

Table of Contents

The Beginning

The morning sun rises slowly over the corn field in front of the farmhouse while crows call to each other in the woods nearby. It is warm this particular morning and the dry tassels on the corn signal that it's almost time for the corn to be broke. The farmhouse is a simple frame construction with a porch across the front. You enter into a large living space with a bedroom on the right. There are two windows in the bedroom, one on the end of the house and one on the front. The wood floors are plank with cracks wide enough to see daylight and the walls are also plank boards, sitting one on top of the other. The large living room has a fireplace on the left. On the back of the house is a door that leads to two small narrow rooms. These two rooms, added as the family grew, are covered by a shed roof, which is simply an extension of the tin roof on the house. One room serves as the kitchen and the other a small bedroom.

Even though the sun is just coming up, the woman of the house is already in the kitchen preparing breakfast. She is 25 years old and petite, about five foot two, she is a pretty woman with dark skin, dark brown hair, and brown eyes. She is barefoot and has on a plain cotton dress and an apron, hand-made by her own two hands. The dress has been altered to cover her large stomach. She is nine months pregnant with her fourth child and expecting to give birth at any time. She is cooking on a wood stove frying fatback in a cast iron frying pan, black from years of use. The homemade biscuits are already in the oven and the grits are sitting on the back of the stove staying warm.

Just as she is finishing the last of the fatback, her husband Clayton walks in through the back door. He has already been down to the barn tending to the chores of feeding the chickens and the hogs, the mule, and two milk cows. He has milked the two cows by hand and has two large buckets of milk. Clayton is a tall man, approximately six foot one, weighing about 175 lbs. He has high cheek bones and a face and hands that show years of hard work outdoors. There is no running water and no indoor plumbing so he pours some water from a metal bucket into a basin and washes his hands. The water must be brought in from a well dug in the yard when they first built the house. It is an open well that was dug by hand. It has a wooden structure built around the top with a rope and bucket for drawing up water.

After Clayton finishes washing his hands he dries them on a towel hanging on a nail and says, "You know Mae, we're gonna have to do something, one of them cows are about to dry up." His wife (whose full name is Mary Mae) is busy putting grits, fatback, and biscuits on a plate for him to eat. After his plate is prepared and set on the table along with a jar of homemade syrup, Mae makes her plate and sits down to eat with him. They each pour a glass of warm fresh milk. The cream is already floating to the top. She will have to churn it into butter soon because there is no refrigeration. They eat silently thinking about the work that must be done. As she finishes her breakfast and before she goes to wake her three children, she ponders all the things that will need to be done around the place before winter sets in. She knows there will be many long hard days ahead to complete everything.

With this Mae gets up from the table and goes to the small bedroom at the rear of the house and wakes up her oldest son Lester, who is seven years old. She then goes to her bedroom which has two double beds in it and wakes up her two girls, Evie, who is five, and her youngest child Alma, who is two and a half years old. Returning to the kitchen, she talks with her husband Clayton about all the things he has to do and suggests they should get the cow with calf again so she would continue producing milk. After their plans are made, Mae returns again to the bedroom and gets Evie and Alma up and dressed. By this time Lester is up and ready to go help his Dad. After feeding the children she cleans up the kitchen and puts the dishes away, hanging the frying pan and pot on a nail in the wall. The two girls go outside to play but not Lester. Clayton needs him to help with the things he is doing. There is always something to do.

Mae begins her day preparing beans from the garden to can. They will be used during the winter and spring until the garden begins to produce again. Her garden is rather large, about 100 x 200 feet. In it she has all kinds of vegetables which she will save for the fall and winter by canning. She is in the process of preparing twenty quarts of her special soup, which has many different ingredients from her garden. The pantry is already well stocked with produce she put up during the summer. It won't be long and it will be time to line things up for butchering the hogs, which is one of their main sources of meat.

Clayton and Lester are busy breaking corn, getting the dried ears off the stalk and tossing them in the wagon pulled by Jenny the mule. This is one smart mule. All Clayton has to do is say "get up" and Jenny will take a few steps until he says "whoa" and she will stop. When the wagon is full they head for the barn where the corn is piled in one corner so it will stay nice and dry. It is also about time to start cutting the sugar cane and making syrup. There is much to be done before winter.

The day is September 10, 1936. It is a pretty day with blue skies and some white clouds hanging about. Mae is into her ninth month and due to give birth at any time and as it was with her first three children, she will give birth at home. It is around ten o clock in the morning, for she has just checked the time on her one and only windup clock, when she feels the first of her birthing pains. She sends one of the girls to go and find her husband and tell him to come quick. She will be assisted by the local midwife, Ms. Annie Wyndham who lives just down the road. The midwife has helped deliver all three of Mae's babies so far, and most every other child in the area of Shulerville, South Carolina, known to the local residents as Hellhole Swamp.

Mae will give birth to a son and will name him Samuel Joseph, straight out of the Bible. This story is about life on the farm where he is born and will grow up, and the lessons he learns along the way. It is also about his family's struggles to make a living off the land through the sweat of their brow. All of these things will shape him and will make him the man, the husband and the Father he will become. This is his life from the beginning into retirement.

3

A PLACE CALLED HELLHOLE SWAMP

****

I am floating in water. It is a strange feeling, one I have never realized before this moment. Something strange is beginning to happen and I have this feeling that things are going to be different. All the liquid I have been floating in is draining away, I am moving and my body is turning with my head down, gravity is pulling me, I am being squeezed, the space I am in is getting smaller and tighter. I have never felt like this before.

I have been here for nine months growing and developing into a male child with very little other changes. Now I am excited, something new is taking place. I see light as I continue my journey head first down towards the light. I stop for a moment; then I move again. Suddenly I feel a hard squeeze and just like that I continue my movement and I see light everywhere. I am not being squeezed anymore, I am free, but I am keeping my eyes closed. Then I feel a sharp slap on my bottom and I gasp and scream and air rushes into my lungs. I take my first breath. I feel I am being moved and turned, something is wiping me, something soft and warm and then I feel pain for the first time. I have just been disconnected from my lifeline that has been nourishing me. From now on I will be on my on to make it in this world or die.

****

From that moment and into my tenth year I grew up on a very rural farm in South Carolina towards the end of the Great Depression (1929 to 1939). It was the worst and longest lasting economic downturn in the history of the United States. My family had very little and lived mostly off what we could grow, raise, catch or hunt. I learned a great deal during those ten years.

Come Go With Me

The place I am from is marked Shulerville on the map, named after Lemuel Shuler who settled there a long time ago. When we lived there, it was known by the locals as "Hellhole Swamp." It is located in northeastern Berkley County, South Carolina, in the middle of the Francis Marion National Forest. Hellhole Swamp is a 2,125 acre swamp that bordered our farm.

The origin of the name Hellhole Swamp is unknown. One theory was the name came from the Revolutionary War when the British had a hard time finding General Francis "Swamp Fox" Marion who used the swamp for cover. Another theory was that the swamp was used by bootleggers during prohibition and they named it "Hellhole." However, the James Cook Map of South Carolina, which predates both time periods noted above, already shows Hellhole Swamp on the map. Therefore, the origin of the name Hellhole Swamp remains a mystery.

To find Hellhole Swamp, look at a map of South Carolina and find Saint Stephens. Then find highway 45 and go northeast towards Jamestown. Yes, there is a Jamestown in South Carolina. You are now in the Francis Marion National Forest. When you reach the intersection of highway 45 and highway 41 you are in Jamestown. It is not much larger now than it was way back then. It even has a Hellhole Swamp Festival each year. Check it out on the web.

Since Jamestown is where I went to school, we will start there and make our way towards where my house used to be. Along the way though, I will show you different places and explain about the people connected to those places as I remember them. The first thing I must tell you is that all the roads were dirt back then and the going was slow.

Staying on highway 45, we will cross over highway 41 then some railroad tracks (those railroad tracks were there then and still are) and just on the right is where my Uncle

David Shuler's grocery store was. As of this writing, some 75 years later, the building is still there. Back then, Uncle David and his wife Lottie (my Mom's sister) lived in a brick house behind the store. The brick house is still there too and their son Oscar stills lives in Jamestown.

Just past the grocery store and on the right was the grammar school I went to as a kid. Below is a picture of my class, third grade I think. That's me in the back row, first one on the left. The school has been torn down and although there had been talk years ago of the town trying to get money to restore it, I guess that never happened. So let's continue on down highway 45 towards the coast. Keep a lookout for Shulerville Road on the right; we're going to turn there.

David Shuler and his wife Lottie's original grocery store

My third grade class
1944

This is where the school was
located

About a half mile before you get to Shulerville Road, take a look to your left; this is where my Uncle Lishe Guerry and his wife lived. Uncle Lishe was married to Lee White, my Mom's sister. Okay, we're coming up on the intersection of highway 45 and Shulerville Road now, so don't forget to turn right. Shulerville Road is also called Highway 49 and will take you to Charleston through a lot of back country. By the way, if you were to continue on highway 45 it would take you to McClellanville on the coast. See page 13 for a map of the area.

There used to be a country store on the right at the intersection of highway 45 and Shulerville Road. It was owned by my Mom's sister, my Aunt Virginia Shuler, and her husband Hurbert. Their son was named Hugie. The store was a large room built on the front of their house. Hurbert was crippled from polio, unable to walk and was in bed most of the time. His bedroom was just behind the store so it was easy for people to step back through the door to say hello and visit with him.

Above is my Uncle Lishe Guerry. He lived back up the road just before Aunt Virginia's store.

It was a typical general store selling the basic things the local community needed. They carried canned goods and basic items such as flour and sugar, some candy, and soft drinks. They also sold gas out front from a hand-crank pump. This pump had a leaver handle with a glass enclosed container at the top. When you worked the leaver back and forth gas would rise in the glass container which was marked off in one gallon increments. If you wanted four gallons, you filled it to that mark, put the hose in your tank and squeezed the handle and the gas would flow by gravity into your tank.

So many things were rationed during World War II and hard to get. I remember special candies such as Almond Joy or Mounds being kept behind the counter for their most important customers only. I always looked forward to going to my Aunt's store. This spot is now a sanitation station.

Across from the store was a building or fertilizer house as they called it, where fertilizer was sold and delivered to the farms in the area. It was run by Lawten and Hugie Shuler, Aunt Virginia's sons. Most of the weekends they had a little card game going on and I heard that Hugie was really good and the big winner most of the time.

Anyway, let's get back to where we were going to take that right turn onto Shulerville Road. Just after the turn go a little piece and on the left you'll see the Pentecostal Holiness Church where our family attended. Just a piece further on the right is where my Uncle Ezra White had his farm. He was in the timber business. All timber sales went through him in Jamestown where it was shipped out by rail. Further down the road on the left is where my Uncle George White, Ezra's brother, had his farm. His son Louis built a house across from George's and still lives there. Ezra and George are my Mom's brothers. Still traveling on Shulerville Road and another one hundred yards down on the right was a little house where my Mom and Dad lived when they first got married. Remember this location when I tell you about how this house came to be.

In a minute we will pass Effie Drive to our right. After you pass Effie Drive look to the right and you'll see where the old Post Office and grist mill were, run by John Bunch and his wife. A house is there now. Another one hundred yards on the left is Fortview Road where the Forts lived. My boyhood friend Alton Fort lived there. Back then Fortview Road went all the way from Shulerville Road to highway 45 but you had to go through two gates to get there. After the Post Office is the New Hope Methodist Church and Cemetery on the right. This is where all the locals were buried and where our youngest sister Vera Elisabeth is buried (more about her birth and death later). From there turn right onto Rhoda Road and go down to the end, it's not very far. At the end and on the right was the home of Lemuel Shuler, the man that Shulerville got its name from. This is the end of Rhoda Road where it ties into Tiger Corner Road. You will see the other end of Tiger Corner Road in a minute, hang in there with me. At this intersection and on the other side of Tiger Corner Road was my Grandfather Edward Lewis's place.

Now let's go back to Shulerville Road and continue. Just after you leave Rhoda Road, on the right was the New Hope School. This school was for all the local children. By the time I started school it had been closed and everyone was being bused to the school in Jamestown. I do remember many of the local women meeting at the old school building and making quilts while we kids played in the yard. I can remember the women sitting around large frames with the quilt attached by the four sides while they hand stitched the patterns in place. I found on the internet that this location was listed as an historical site but no sign has been put up to that effect. I bet the swastika quilt I will mention later was made there.

Further on you will intersect with the other end of Tiger Corner Road (I told you that you would see it again). At the intersection of Tiger Corner Road and Shulerville Road on the left there was an old house when I was a child, I don't remember whose house it was, but I do remember looking in through the window and seeing a guitar leaning in the corner even though there was no one living there at that time. The house would have been about where Swampfield Road is now.

Just past Tiger Corner Road there were two streams, the first was Echau Creek and the next was called Mungdam Creek. There used to be a large amount of water at Mungdam Creek because I remember my Dad stopping on the bridge, diving in and going swimming there. Mungdam is not much of a creek now because a pond has been built behind our old home place which has restricted the water flow to a trickle. Just across the creek on the left is where the Hazelton's lived. My older brother Lester was good friends with their son

Kenneth. Almost directly across the road from the Hazelton's lived our school bus driver Mr. Patz and his wife Lizzie. They were Germans and this is the lady that influenced my Mom in making a swastika designed quilt. My wife Kay still has that quilt. When the quilt was made, Nazis Germany was on the rise.

The swastika is a very old symbol that has been used for over 3,000 years and artifacts such as pottery and coins from ancient times had this design. It was a commonly used symbol as far back as 1000 BC but was called by different names. Nazis Germany called it the swastika and under its banner used it to murder millions of people.

The photo above shows where the Post Office
and grist mill were located

New Hope Methodist Church

This is my wife Kay's remembrance of the quilt:

"MaaMaa" (that's Sam's Mother) gave it to us right
after we got married and I think it was one she made. The
underside shows where an iron was placed on it and burned
through. I was the one that did it and the patch is in the
shape of the sole of the iron and not even done in a square.
That goes to show how inexperienced I was at fixing things
like that (I was only about 22 then).

11

I remember it being done when I was expecting "Jink" (Jeanne, who is our youngest daughter). Sam and I, our two daughters Sammie Kay and LaDonna were in Tampa Florida for six weeks while Sam was working at Stovall Fixture Company. We had rented a house for the six weeks and I was using a bed to press something with the quilt as a base. Somehow the iron got placed face down while it was hot. I was in another part of the house so maybe one of the two girls knocked it over since it was on the foot of the bed. When I went back into the bedroom it was literally smoldering with fire sparks showing on the fabric so I poured a little water on it to put it out. Not even sure if Sam knows all this or remembers. LOL.

I remember flipping the mattress over and hiding the burned iron shape. I think it even burned through the padding on the mattress that belonged to the woman (we rented the house furnished). Maybe you have already seen it but next time ya'll are down, take a look at the quilt. This is another one of the family adventures to store away in your memory banks."

Okay, that's what Kay remembers, now back to my story. .

So, let's get back to where we left off on Shulerville Road. A little farther up the road from the two creeks you'll see School Bus Drive on the left. Back then, School Bus Drive used to take you to Honey Hill and back to highway 45 again. Anyway, after you turn onto School Bus Drive, on the left is where Lloyd Lewis lived, my Father's cousin. Now go back out to Shulerville Road and we will continue going down the road. After you pass School Bus Drive, the next road on the right is Popa Road; go ahead and turn there. After making the turn you'll see where the local midwife, Ms. Annie Wyndham lived (we always pronounced it Windom). It's just there on the right. For those of you who don't know, a midwife helps other women have their children. Back then there was no doctor in the area.

We lived at the end of Popa Road in a two room house, where I was conceived and born. There are several houses there now.

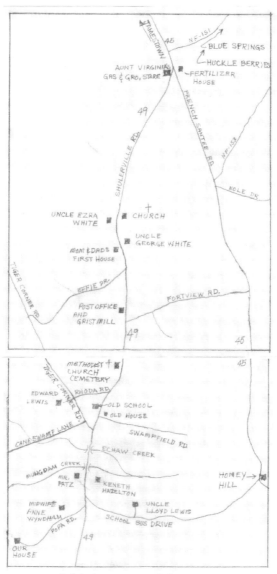

This is a map of the area.

Where We Lived: The Farm & The Family

When we lived there, just after you crossed a small drainage ditch there was a fence and a gate. After you entered the gate there was a field on the left. To the right under a big oak tree was the sugar cane mill and just past the mill was one barn. Down from this barn was another barn and a fenced in area for the cows. In front of that was our garden and our house. The house was nothing fancy. It had a front porch where we all used to sit in the summer time and visit or where Mom and Dad would cut hair to make a little cash. A small kitchen was on the rear of the house. Of course, the house was added on to as the family grew.

One time Dad added a small room on the back next to the kitchen large enough to sleep two. Later, Dad had to expand again, this time adding a new kitchen and another bedroom at the left end of the house. I don't remember where I slept as a baby, but I do remember sleeping in the larger bedroom when I got bigger. Just out from this room and kitchen was a well that was the only source of water until the kitchen was added. Dad had a hand pump put in when he built the kitchen. Over from the well I remember a really big oak tree that had a rope hanging down for swinging. We all had a lot of fun on that swing. Beyond the tree was a shed we called the chicken house. I don't know why because one end was open. I do remember Mom and the girls using it for a bathroom though. The boys went where ever they were at the time. Out back there was a large field with a drainage ditch separating it from another field. On the other side of these fields was the swamp where the area got its name.

All of our close relatives lived in this area of Shulerville. Referred to as Hellhole Swamp, it consisted of eleven different families with names such as White, Lewis, Guerry, Shuler, Bunch, Fort, Patz and Hazelton.

I was born September 10, 1936. I was the middle child of three brothers and three sisters. The oldest to youngest was Lester, Evie, Alma, me, Furman, Mendel and Vera. Lester was four years older than Evie and the rest of us were about two to three years apart. Vera, the youngest, died at about three months old from a head trauma received when she was born. She was the only child born in a hospital.

The story is when it became time for the baby to be born Daddy took Mom to Charleston to the hospital. When they got there they had to get a doctor. As they waited, Mom began to have the baby but the nurses did not want the birth to happen until the doctor got there. We think the baby was in the birth canal when the nurses pushed Mom's legs together saying "You don't want to have this baby until the Doctor gets here" and damaged the baby's head. Vera was not right from the beginning. She lived for three months and began having convulsions and died.

I remember in the big bedroom there was a large metal trunk at the window between the two beds. Little Vera was placed in a basket on the trunk during the wake when the neighbors came over to pay their respects. Afterward, everyone went to the cemetery for the funeral and the burial.

There was no funeral home. The local people dug the hole and handled the burial. I remember the little box being let down with ropes and the grave being filled in. The dirt was mounded up and they packed it down with a long board, rounding the sides and the ends to make it look pretty. Then we all went home.

Mom thought she should never have gone to the hospital. She also thought she was being punished because she had not wanted another child. It took Mom a long time to recover because of her guilt in not wanting another child. My two younger brothers and I remember hearing a moaning sound for several weeks coming from the wall where the trunk sat. We figured it was Vera's spirit. Mom did not have any more children.

The land we lived on had been given to my Daddy in 1931 by his Dad, Edward Lewis, whose property joined to the north. Edward Lewis got his land from his Dad, James

Whiteford Lewis. The land to the east was owned by Ms. Annie Wyndham, the midwife. The south side joined an old railroad that used to run from Charleston up past Honey Hill.

I do recall there was a field in this area separated by woods from the rest of our property. I was under the impression that it was a field Daddy leased. This land could have belonged to the railroad? To the west was Hellhole Swamp. Mungdam Creek flowed out of the swamp towards the northeast. The people living at our old home place now have built a large pond that takes in all the water that flows from Mungdam Creek.

Daddy built this house about 1934 and began farming. According to the survey the total land at that time was thirty-six acres and about seven acres of this was swamp land. Some of this land was cleared and had been fields used by my grandfather Edward Lewis. Daddy did open up some more fields by removing trees and digging up the stumps. Below, I list tax receipts to show what property values were and how hard it was to pay the taxes.

In 1930, the property value on 36 acres was $30 and taxes were $5.50. In 1937, the property value on 36 acres was $100 and taxes were paid June 1, 1938. The back taxes were $17.80 plus $1.25 penalty. For 1938 and 1939, taxes show an additional 20 acres but I'm not sure where this land joined the existing 36 acres or how Dad got it, but I'm guessing he got it from his father Edward. The 1938 and 1939 taxes were paid in February of 1942. Total back taxes were $25.48 for the 56 acres. The 1940 to 1942 taxes were paid on time but 1943 and 1944 taxes were not paid until January of 1945. The 1945 taxes were paid in January of 1946. Note: We moved to Rock Hill, South Carolina in 1946 but the farm was not sold for a couple of years.

Dad built a house in Rock Hill, South Carolina in 1948 and those taxes were paid in December of 1949. We rented a place through the winter of 1946 and part of the year of 1947 until that house was finished.

The Shulerville, South Carolina farm taxes for 1946 were paid in 1947; taxes for 1947 were paid in April of 1948; and taxes for 1948 were paid in October of 1948. Taxes for

1949 were paid in December of 1949 and taxes for 1949 were paid on the farm in January of 1951.

Later in this story, I will tell you about moving and selling the farm. We moved and about three years later the farm was sold to a Mr. Gaston. I have no information on what it sold for. I feel he probably cut and sold enough timber to pay for it.

The two photos below were taken in Shulerville, S.C.

Clayton Lewis and wife Mae at Wilson Mims birthday celebration, circa 1941. Photo courtesy of Ernest W. Mims.

Mom & Dad -1941.
Mom was 30, Dad 34

Mom & Dad – 1946.

Left: Mom and Dad around 1947 after we moved to Rock Hill, S.C.
Center: My grandfather Edward Lewis, my Dad's father.
Right: Caroline Elizabeth Mills, my Mom's mother.
(See more family pictures at the back of this book).

This is a picture of my Uncle Cordie Lewis, my father's brother, and his wife Alice around 1945. He joined the Air Force about this time and she stayed with us for a while until Uncle Cordie found out where he would be stationed.

I remember Uncle Cordie coming back from the war to visit. When we ran out to see who had driven up at the house, he made a remark to me I have never forgotten. He said "You look like a taxi cab with both doors open." His reference was to my ears which were rather large. At the time I did not know what a taxi was, but I knew he was referring to my ears, so I have always remembered what he said. Funny how things like that will stay with you all of your life. Big ears were not my only problem growing up. I also had issues with my teeth. I will explain more about that in my teen years.

Look at those ears

In the early days, Daddy raised cows, mostly for milk and butter and he raised hogs too. We would kill hogs in the fall of the year. The meat was preserved in a lot of ways. One way was to salt cure the hams and shoulders or smoke cure them. Other parts would be ground up and made into sausages. Almost everything we used was raised or grown on the farm. Corn for grits and corn meal, hogs for ham, fatback, sausage, lard for cooking and cracklings left from making the lard. The only thing that we did not grow was flour and sugar. These two were not used that much because Mom would use syrup to sweeten things and bread was mostly cornbread. She did have to buy flour for biscuits or to make a cake. Back in those days, people even made their own soap, which reminds me of something else I wanted to share.

I have been told that I had a skin rash as an infant and it must have itched terribly. My dad got so upset with me one time that he picked me up by my legs and was tempted to bash my head against the fire place. This may be what prompted my Mom to take me to see a doctor in McClellanville. The doctor said I had eczema and washing me was the worst thing she could do. So from that point on I became the dirtiest kid in the house. She also applied some sort of cream to the rash and slowly I got better. You know, I just thought of something, I just mentioned that in the early days people made their own soap. I bet Mom was using lye soap when she washed me and that's what caused the rash. I had not thought of that before.

I have also been told about the time when I was a toddler and went out in back of the house to where Daddy kept his honey bees. Remember now, I was a very inquisitive little fellow and had to check out everything. I must have gone over to check them out and the bees did not like what I was doing and began to sting me so I screamed and Daddy came running. I have been told the bees had me completely covered and Dad grabbed me up and started brushing off the bees. That many stings should have killed me but it didn't so there must have been more in my life to be done.

I heard stories about moonshine and the times during the Depression when no money was to be had. My

Mom said that times were so tough everyone made moonshine. They would sell the moonshine to people from some of the big cities to get a little spending money. Everybody sold moonshine, except the preacher, and he would let you put your still on his land if you would feed the corn mash to his hogs.

The sheriff was always trying to catch my Dad and his friends but mostly they would get away. The still would be smashed but it wouldn't be long and they would have another set up and operating. Dad told us of the times when some fancy dude would show up with his big car and they would load it up with moonshine. There was good money to be made off moonshine but the risk of getting caught kept getting higher and higher so Daddy finally gave it up, after getting caught.

The story goes like this. Before Mom and Dad got married, Dad was making moonshine with his soon to be brother-in-law Frank White and Mom's cousin Barney Bird. Daddy must have been making lots of money because when he asked Mom to marry him and she said yes, he hired some fellows to build him a house. This house was not a big thing, about four rooms, a living room, a kitchen and two bedrooms. The land he had it built on belonged to Mom; she had inherited it from her Father. In fact, most of the land in the area belonged to the Whites and the Lewis land joined to the southwest and that is where Daddy had his still. Daddy's Grandfather, James Whiteford Lewis, originally bought the land from Mom's uncle, George Washington White.

My dad had been doing this for a while, selling the moonshine to someone in Charlotte, North Carolina. Once the deal had been made the man in Charlotte would send somebody to pick up the moonshine at a prearranged spot. You see, nobody met with anyone after the deal was struck. The man making the pick-up left the money at a secret place where Daddy could get it later. This reduced the risk of getting caught.

One day after Mom and Dad had been married for a while, Dad and his brother-in-law were working the still while Barney was off doing something else and Dad saw someone walking in the woods as if they were hunting. Dad thought something looked funny so he walked over to his brother-in-law and said "Don't look, but when I tell you to run, you go that way and I will go this way." He also told him "If you get caught, do not tell the law who owns the still." With that, Dad told him to run and they took off in different directions.

Well, Dad ended up going to his house where after a while the law showed up and arrested him for making moonshine. You see, his brother-in-law had been caught and the law had said to him, "If you tell us who owns the still, we will let you go." He told them, but they didn't let him go, he ended up in jail and served six months. Dad ended up hiring a lawyer and got off with a six hundred dollar fine. Six hundred dollars back then was a lot of money so they must have been making a lot. Frank sent word to Dad to come bail him out of jail, but Dad refused because Frank had told the law who owned the still. Dad did take care of Frank's wife, Danie, while Frank was in jail for those six months.

Dad, Frank White and Barney Bird had the still for several years already and it was during this time that Mom and Dad had their first two children, Lester and Evie. However, Dad decided since he had such a close call with the law, and was now married and starting a family he had best give up making moonshine. He must have sold the house he built to pay the fine because he ended up asking his father for some land and was given the property.

Dad and his friends cut trees and then had it sawed into lumber to build a house. Cutting trees wasn't easy back then, there was no such thing as a chain saw. They used a big saw about six feet long with handles on both ends, pulled back and forth by two people. The saw was constantly getting gummed up by sap from the trees. This was especially true when cutting pine trees. To keep this from happening, they would always have a glass drink bottle with turpentine in it. They had pine needles stuck in the top so they could shake out some turpentine on the saw to keep it from sticking.

Anyway, once the house was completed, they moved in and started farming. That land and house is where I was born. My brother Lester told me after they had been living there for a while trying to make a living farming that Dad set up another still, but before he started making liquor he decided that since he was now a father he had better quit the liquor business for good. Later as new fields were needed the process was the same. Cut the trees and use what you could for lumber and burn the rest. The stumps had to be dug up by hand and a mule would drag them to the burn area. This process was called breaking new ground. My earliest recollection is when an area back near the swamp was cleared. I was right there helping drag limbs and brush to where things were burned.

During the Depression, times were very hard. Dad would hand cut railroad cross ties for 50 cents a piece. First, he and Lester would cut a tree down and saw it into the proper length then he used an ax-like blade to flatten each side. The blade was about 12 inches long with a curved point on the end. The point was used to hook in the log to turn it over so he could flatten another side. When he had one completed he would take the mule and hook a chain to the cross tie so the mule could pull it out to the road. Every once in a while the railroad would have a truck come and pick up the cross ties and take them to Jamestown where they would be loaded and taken to wherever the railroad had need of them. I'm sure other men in the area were cutting cross ties too. I also remember Dad talking about working on the W.P.A. (Work Projects Administration). This was a government run work program doing work along the roads, clearing brush, repairing ditches, etc. It was a program to give people something to do, to make a person feel useful and to earn a little money.

When the United States entered World War II in 1941, I was 5 years old and I remember Dad going to work at the navy yard in Charleston, South Carolina. Everyone was needed for the war effort. The Navy yard was constantly repairing, building or loading ships. I'm not sure what job Dad had but he had regular money coming in. I remember one Friday night when he came home (he had had just a little too much to drink) with a bag and two dresses for my sisters. I remember him saying when he gave the dresses to them, "Your Daddy works at the Navy yard". He was so proud that he could afford to buy them something from a store instead of Mom having to make it.

One time Daddy came in from working at Navy yard with an alligator tied across the front bumper. The gator had been lying on the black road getting warm late that evening when Dad and the other men he worked with were coming home. Well, they stopped the car and killed the alligator and brought it home, it was food. I remember Mom cooking the steaks from the tail and it was wiggling in the frying pan. Frog legs do that too, it has something to do with the nerves.

We didn't have electricity, we used kerosene lamps. For heat in the wintertime we had one fireplace and we heated with wood. At night when the fire went out there was no heat in the house at all. The floor boards in our bedroom had cracks between the boards big enough that you could see through. Before going to bed at night my younger brothers and I would take a blanket or quilt made by our Mom and stand in front of the fireplace and get it nice and warm then we would run and jump in the bed and wrap ourselves in that warm blanket and go to sleep.

I remember my Mom and Dad cutting hair on the front porch on Friday and Saturday night (I think they charged 25 cents for a haircut). Since there was no electricity, they used hand operated clippers to cut hair and kerosene lamps to see, but it was difficult to see with those kinds of lamps. One day my Daddy came home with a gas lantern that used the same kind of gas you use in your car. You would put the gas in the lantern and pump it up. When you opened the valve a very fine mist of gas would come out onto the wick, except this was not a flat wick, but a little bag that looked like a tiny fish net. This little bag had a drawstring in the top and it was put around the opening in the lantern and the string was pulled tight. When the bag was new it had to be lit with a match and the little bag would burn up and all that was left were ashes but it did not fall apart, it would open up into a nice round circle. I have no idea what this material was but when you turned on the gas you could light the wick and it would glow real bright. You had to be careful not to touch the bag with the match though because if you did a hole would come in it, and then if the lantern was bumped the bag would fall apart. We got along just fine though because no one stayed out very long after dark and went to bed early. That's how the saying "going to bed with the chickens" got started.

When neighbors from the area would come to our place to get their hair cut, they used this as a chance to visit and keep up with what was happening in the area. I remember the time when Lloyd Lewis came over one Saturday night to get his hair cut. He always rode a real pretty horse. I can see him now prancing down the road coming to the house. That night you could tell he had had a little too much to drink by the way he rode and when he got down off the horse he fell down and had to be helped up. He hung around though and eventually got his hair cut.

Water on the farm was from an enclosed well where we had a bucket and a rope so water could be drawn from the well. When this house was first built we used this particular well for drinking and for washing clothes. In the hot summertime, since we had no refrigeration, Mom would keep jars of milk and butter down in the well where it was cool. She had a rope or heavy string tied to the top so she could let the jars down into the cool water.

We only took a bath once a week, usually on Saturday, so we could be nice and clean to go to church on Sunday. Mom had a big wash tub and that is where we took our baths. All of the kids went bare footed during the summertime and only got a pair of shoes for the winter.

We had two barns. In one we kept corn, as well as hay up in the loft. The area out front was fenced in for the milk cows. The other barn near the cane mill was where we also kept hay. It had shed roofs on the side and front with one area for the mule Jenny and the other for the wagon.

At one point the house was extended and a new kitchen and bedroom were added. I remember Daddy making forms for the support pillars and pouring the concrete. He already had lumber prepared and stacked out in front of the house. My brother Furman and I would use a board that stuck out from the others as a spring board. We would jump up and down and go flying into the air and land on the ground. We found all kinds of ways to have fun.

Once the rooms were complete a platform was added outside the kitchen door. A well was drilled and a pump installed. It was the first time we had running water, which meant pumping the handle and the water would run out. Sometimes the water would drain back down the pipe and you would have to prime the pump. To do this you would pour some water down into the pump to get it started pumping again. With the new pump we could get water and not have to go to the well. The problem with this pump water was it had so much iron in it you could not get soap to lather. We only used it for drinking. The water from the well was used for washing clothes and keeping things cool.

After the new kitchen and bedroom were added Mom and Dad had a big party in the kitchen. We little kids would sneak up to the door from the living room and listen at what was going on. They sure were having a good time with music playing and dancing. When it was all complete Lester and I stayed in the new bedroom, Evie and Alma in the little room on the back of the house with Furman and Mendel in one of the double beds in the big bedroom with Mom and Dad.

We spent most of our time doing chores like going and getting eggs the chickens had laid or down to the barn to feed the cows or 'slop' the hogs (that's what they called feeding the hogs). In fact, we had a bucket in the kitchen and all of the scraps (leftover food) were dumped in the bucket and fed to the hogs.

There wasn't any grass to cut back in those days. The yard was mostly sand because the soil where we lived was very sandy. Occasionally Mom would make us sweep the yard with what they call a yard broom. It was made up of branches to create a broom with a real brushy bottom. Sweeping of the yard was mainly to get rid of sticks and leaves that had fallen from the trees in the wintertime. Sometimes this yard broom was put to another use if we did wrong. You got it, we were thrashed with it.

When Mom needed some more vegetables from the garden, we would be sent to get them. The garden was plowed to get everything set up for planting, after that it was all done by hand with a hoe. We all spent many hours working in the garden and grew lots of things on the farm. We had corn, sugar cane, oats, velvet beans, water melons, plus all the things our Mama planted in the garden; every kind of vegetable you can imagine. She planted all kinds of beans and vegetables, carrots, squash, cucumbers, radishes, tomatoes, lettuce and cabbage. The cantaloupes and watermelons were planted out back in the field next to the corn and sugar cane. Things that could be canned were put up in glass jars and sealed for future use. Mama was real proud of her garden.

We also grew regular potatoes (the kind you make mashed potatoes from) and sweet potatoes. For those of you who don't know, potatoes grow in the ground under a bush and have to be dug up out of the ground. Sweet potatoes and regular potatoes were kept differently. The house we lived in was set up on blocks so you could crawl under the house. It stayed nice and dry under there so when the regular potatoes were dug out of the ground and dried off, we would spread paper on the ground under the house and put the potatoes on it so they would not go bad.

When the sweet potatoes were dug up and had dried good, we would take a shovel and build up a place with dirt about six feet square and about ten inches high. We would then put a thick layer of pine needles on this dirt and stack up the sweet potatoes in a pointed pile shaped like a cone. Then we would put pine needles over all the potatoes and pile dirt up over the pine needles. That way when it rained the water would run down the sides and not get into the potatoes and get them wet, because if they got wet they would rot. When Mom needed some, we would go out to this pile and dig a hole in the top, take out some potatoes and put the pine needles back in and cover them up with dirt. Mom kept a bucket in the house and kept the potatoes there. When she needed more we would go fill the bucket again. The bucket-full would last maybe a week. We ate a lot of potatoes.

When it was time to plant corn the field had to be plowed and prepared by plowing furrows and piling the dirt into rows. The seeds were then planted about twelve inches apart in the furrow. As the corn grew some of the dirt piled along either side was pulled in around the corn. This was done by hand with a hoe. If you used the mule and plow too early the dirt would knock over the corn and cover it. Once the corn reached about knee high we would pull the dirt around it one last time. This was called "laying by" and would be done with the mule and plow. By this time, all the dirt on either side of the corn was pulled up around the corn, so now the pile and the furrow had switched places. The act of moving dirt up around the corn also kept the weeds from growing.

When the corn reached a point where the tassels came out of the top, it was time for magic to happen. When a light wind would blow, the little tiny seeds from the tassels would be blown all over the place and some would fall down and get trapped in the leaf right where the leaf joins the stalk. It would lay there and when the dew in the morning settled on the leaves some would run down to the seed and it would sprout and grow into an ear of corn. When the ear had grown to full size, Mama would break some of the corn and we would have corn on the cob. The corn was tender and sweet. She would also cut the grains off the cob and put it up in jars so we could have fresh corn anytime.

Once the corn had completely matured and dried we would break the corn off the stalks one at a time and pile them in the wagon. Then they were taken to the barn and piled in one area of the barn. As corn was needed it had to be shucked (that's where you pull the leaves off) and the grains rubbed off the cob. When done by hand this could be real tough on your hands because corn has sharp points when it is dry and hard. Sometimes people would hold an ear in one hand and use a corn cob in the other and rub the cob across the corn and rub the grains off. Daddy finally bought a corn sheller. Once the ear of corn had been shucked you could push the ear down into a spring loaded hole while turning a handle at the same time. A wheel with little spikes sticking out would rub the corn off. The grains of corn went into a bucket and the cob came out a different place. Corn cobs had many uses, one of which was toilet paper.

Some of the corn was used to feed the cows, horses and hogs, although mostly they ate hay and slop. When we wanted grits or cornmeal we took a bag of shelled corn to the local mill, which was about four miles away. They would grind it into grits and some into corn meal. Most people having very little money would pay the mill person by giving them some of the corn. The amount was determined by how much you had ground. The cornmeal was used for making corn bread and was also used to coat fish before frying. Corn bread was used a lot because if we wanted biscuits we had to buy flour. By the way, our Momma used lard for all her cooking including making biscuits, and she used syrup that we made from sugar cane to sweeten things. I will tell you about the sugar cane later. We did have problems though with bugs called boll weevils chewing little holes into the grains of corn, and the grits cooked by our Momma always had little black specs in it. You're right, it was those boll weevils.

As I said, our Momma grew all kinds of garden vegetables but back in those days, besides the boll weevils, there were a lot of wild animals. The animals would come into the garden and eat up her stuff so Mom and Dad had a big high fence around the whole garden. The high fence was to keep the deer out and around the bottom of the fence they had another fence about two and a half feet high. This fence was made of small wire so that small animals such as rabbits could not get through the holes. The sweet potatoes were planted just outside the garden, because if the animals came and ate the sweet potato vines it didn't make any difference, because the sweet potatoes grew on the roots in the ground. At the end of the growing season some of the beans were left to dry on the bush so they could be used as seed the next year. Watermelon and cantaloupe seeds were laid out to dry and used for the next planting. All of the seeds were kept in closed jars to keep bugs from getting into them. There were times when new seeds had to be purchased though.

Sweet and regular potatoes would be used to replant by cutting off the sprouts, or eyes as we called them, and put them in the ground so a new vine or bush would grow. Some things such as turnips would be left in the ground so the tops would go to seed. Some sugar cane and grains of corn were set aside for the same reason. The corn had to be picked through to make sure that each grain did not have any insects or boll weevils in them because if they did, nothing would be left come spring time.

Mom was a very good cook and we always had vegetables from the garden or things she had canned. Mom's specialty was a mixture called bean soup. It was made from lima beans, corn, okra and tomatoes all seasoned with fatback. We also ate different types of meat which was either cured/salted pork or fresh meat we had killed from hunting.

Left to right: Our first cousin Warren White, Furman, me, and Mendel. This picture was taken around 1945 in our yard in Shulerville, South Carolina. I am about nine years old. This deer got in the garden through a hole in the fence when it was very small and we kept it as a pet. In this picture it is sucking on a bottle. That is the front porch of our house in the background.

We hunted the year round. Squirrel, deer, turkey, dove, quail, rabbit, fish, whatever, it all went into the pot. We had no refrigeration so when it was brought home it was cooked and eaten. We also ate a lot of rice, which she had to buy. She prepared it in many ways but one of my favorites was after the men had gone hunting, usually for squirrels. They would always bring whatever they shot and killed back to the house to clean. I have always had trouble skinning a squirrel but my Dad and these men could have the skin off before you knew it. They would take the skin off the head down to the shoulders, then grab the head and pull the hide down and off the back legs just like that. Then it was washed and the meat cut into pieces.

Our Mom would make a dish called squirrel perlo. She would put the squirrel meat in water and bring it to a boil; this is called parboiling and is done to make the meat tender. The meat was then salted, rolled in flour and placed in a frying pan to brown and brown only. She would put rice in a pot with water and put the squirrel meat in with the rice and simmer or cook the rice. When our Mom cooked rice like this it was always kind of wet and moist. In other words, she didn't cook it dry. This would make the squirrel meat real tender and of course the flour that had been browned on the meat would flavor the rice and turn it all light brown. This particular dish was a favorite of mine and the whole family.

The thing that was interesting about this perlo rice is that she put the head of the squirrel in with the rest of the meat. Now the squirrel's head had been skinned and cleaned but the eyes and the teeth were still in the skull. I remember Mom and Dad taking out one of the heads and with a spoon they would crack the skull open and eat the brains. I don't recall me or my brothers and sisters trying this but apparently it was very good. In those days, most parts of the animal were eaten.

We also ate beef tripe which is the stomach of a cow. It's about one quarter inch thick and is made up of several layers of stringy meat or muscle running in different directions. One layer runs in one direction and then another layer on top of that runs in the opposite direction. This gives the stomach of a cow a lot of room to expand as they eat grass. Mom would cut the tripe into three inch squares, then flour and fry it. The first time I tried it I didn't like it. It was so stringy I was unable to chew it. Of course my teeth had

31

not developed properly and that made chewing it difficult. After that first time, I don't think I ever tried it again. Now chitlins is something I do not remember my Momma cooking, maybe because she knew where they came from and what used to be in them.

One other thing she cooked was cakes and pies. She used fruit from her own fruit trees (apple, pear, and peach) or wild berries she had picked. I remember going with her and some of the other women from the area to a place near Blue Springs to pick blueberries, we called them huckleberries (I've been told that Blue Springs is a nudist camp now). Anyway, we went in through a pine forest and came out into a big clearing with berry bushes higher than the women's heads and Mom said, "See that dead pine tree?" which was right where we came in. She said "If you get lost, just come back to that tree." Those bushes were loaded with berries and by the time we left, they had buckets full. Mom made a lot of delicious things with these berries but one of our favorites was blueberry cobbler. At times like that living on the farm wasn't all that bad.

Games, Dogs, Snakes & Medical Treatments

My brothers and I were always barefooted in the summertime. We only got a pair of shoes from the Sears catalog when winter came. Well, one summer day we were out running and playing a little game we called rabbit and dog. One of us would be picked to be the rabbit and the other two would be the dogs. Now you could have more than two dogs, you could have three of four kids run and be dogs, but only one person could be the rabbit. When we played rabbit and dog, we would run down trails in the woods. We knew all the trails where we ran so while the dogs would be right behind, the person playing the rabbit would be in front trying to turn onto another trail to lose the dogs. We had a lot of fun doing this.

One particular day I was the rabbit and was running along a trail. All of a sudden I put my foot down right on a snake and when I felt the snake move I jumped so fast the snake didn't even have time to bite me. It was a copperhead that I had stepped on because I recognized the snake when I turned around and looked at it. My two brothers, Furman (who we called "Tibby") and Mendel (who we called "M.L.") came running up but the snake had gone into a hole in a stump. We got sticks to try and kill him but we never were able to get him out of the stump.

We had different kinds of snakes around there, and plenty of them. There were copperheads, cottonmouth moccasins, and even rattlesnakes. We had a dog named Fido who just loved to kill snakes. One time a black snake had just come out of where the chickens had their nest and you could tell he had eaten an egg because you could see the bulge in the snake. Well, Fido spied him and came running, but Fido had a special way he killed snakes. He would start barking and going round and round the snake, then he would stop and lay still. This made the snake start to crawl away and that's when

Fido would get him. He would lunge in and grab the snake in the middle and start shaking his head, which kept the snake from biting him. Then he would throw the snake down and back off. He would look to see if the snake was dead and if he wasn't, he would grab him and shake him again. He would continue doing this until the snake was dead. Well, this time when he started shaking the snake, the egg came out just a flying. It hit the side of the house, smashing it, and the yellow part dripped all down the side of the house. Living and playing in all those woods near our house; how we never got a snake bite, I will never know. Now the real dogs did get bit sometimes and when that happened our Momma would mix up her special remedy, sulfur and syrup, then give it to the dogs and they always survived. If we got a snake bite, that's probably what we would have gotten too.

There was another time when our Daddy told us to go and cut some fresh oats, it was used to feed the mules and cows and stuff. Well, when we went out there to cut some down we also cut paths to play in. One Sunday morning Daddy heard Fido out there just a barking so he got his gun (he always took his gun when he went out like that) and went to find out what was going on. When he got out there he realized the commotion was in the oats field so he went on over to see what was going on. Wouldn't you know it, Fido had a big old rattlesnake cornered in the field right where we had been cutting paths to play. Fido and the snake had been going round and round until the oats were laid flat all over the place. When our Daddy saw the snake he was startled; this was the biggest rattlesnake he had ever seen. This snake was so big that even Fido had kept his distance. Fido was a very smart dog and knew he couldn't kill that rattlesnake like he did other snakes.

Daddy shot and killed the big old snake and took it to the edge of the field and went back home to get ready for church (we always went to church) and at church the story was told and everyone marveled at how we three little boys didn't get bit. That afternoon many of the neighbors from other farms came over to see this big snake. There were no Doctors or hospitals around so if one of us had been bitten, we would have been goners for sure, or maybe Mom's special remedy would have saved us.

We three boys did a lot of things for fun and we did it with common every day things around the farm. We would use a pitch fork (sometimes called a hay fork) to play with. A pitch fork had four sharp tines and was used to get the hay and pitch or throw the hay out of the barn to the cows. We would take the fork with the prongs turned up and slide it along the ground walking behind it like we were driving a truck or something. One day Furman, not watching where he was going while sliding the fork, ran right into the back of his younger brother Mendel and stuck the sharp end of one of the prongs in his heel. Boy you should have heard the hollering. Furman got a good whipping for that one. There were other things we did for fun, or tried to do, such as standing on the ground in front of our house and peeing up trying to hit the tin roof on the front porch. What pressure we had back then.

The nearest Doctor was about thirty miles away in McClellanville on the coast. Jamestown was about twelve miles away but at that time there was no Doctor there. With no Doctor nearby, we made do with home remedies. Sulfur and cane syrup for snake bites (mostly for the dogs like I said before as I don't remember any of us getting bitten by a snake) and if you got cut by anything rusty, you would soak it in kerosene.

One time, I was standing up in the back of our old truck not holding on while my older brother was driving. We had been out cutting wood and the old crosscut saw was in the back with the teeth turned up in the air. When my brother put on brakes, you guessed it, I fell forward and my right wrist went straight down on the saw. It cut through the skin and scratched the tendons running to my hand. To this day I have a scar that resembles stitches, but I never got any stitches. My Mom bent my wrist forward so the cut would stay closed and bandaged it that way. The wrinkles where she had my hand bent to keep the cut closed are what appear now as stitches.

Another day, Mom, my sisters, and my younger brothers Furman and Mendel, and I were in the wagon on our way to the store at Honey Hill. Furman, who was about three years old, was reaching over the side with his hand slapping the spokes of the wheel as it turned. At one point he must have grabbed one of the spokes, because faster than you can say "watch out" he went out of the wagon head first and landed on his back and the back wheel of the wagon rolled right over his stomach. He must not have been hurt though because he jumped right up and ran to catch up with the wagon.

When I was about six or seven we were going somewhere in Dad's old car. As we were leaving the farm, I stayed on the running board so I could open the gate to let us out. Before Dad completely stopped the car, I jumped off to get the gate and slipped when my feet hit the soft sand. My leg went under the car and the back wheel went right over it. I didn't get hurt though, I guess because the soft sand cushioned my leg. Another time I recall jumping up and down on the bed. The bed was near the wall and had an iron railing on the sides to hole the slats and the springs. My right leg went down between the wall and the railing and the metal railing scraped the skin off right down to the bone about half way between the ankle and the knee. I still have the scar to prove it.

Stepping on rusty nails wasn't a problem either. Mama had a remedy for that too. What happened in this instance is that my two younger brothers, Furman and Mendel, and I made some stilts to walk around on. We of course had to make our own, so we took some strips of wood and nailed blocks on them for our bare feet to rest on, remember we went bare foot all summer long. We would then get up on these stilts and walk around. Most of the fun was in making them. Well, one day when I was on my stilts the block pulled off the strip and when my foot came down it landed smack on the nail and stuck way up in the bottom of my foot. I remember sitting down and having to pull the block with the nail from my foot. The old nail was rusty so my Mom had me soak my foot in kerosene. I hobbled around for a while but it eventually healed. God really looked after us during those times.

Although Mom and Dad used their own home remedies they also followed a lot of the old passed down remedies for one ailment or another. I remember when I had a sore throat they made me pee in a can and then tried to make me drink it, but I refused. In fact, I was just talking with my two sisters in June 2011 about this and they said that Mom and Dad made them do the same thing. You must remember though, they were doing it out of love.

Making Syrup from Sugar Cane

The sugar cane we grew (we called it cane) looked a lot like bamboo except it was a reddish brown color. It grew to six or seven feet tall, and would be about one inch in diameter. We always saved cane from the year before to start new plants. The cane stalk had joints every six to seven inches and we would cut the joints off and plant them. New cane would sprout from each joint and grow another stalk, but you could also lay the whole stalk in the ground to get new cane plants. After it had matured, usually around September, we would go down through the field with the wagon. The leaves were stripped off the cane with blades made of hard pine wood shaped like a machete and fairly sharp on one side. Someone else would follow behind with a real big sharp knife and chop off the top, then cut it off near the ground. The cane was piled in the wagon until it was full, and off it went to the cane mill.

If you took a knife and peeled the outer layer off of the cane, the area between the joints was kind of firm. We would do this then cut a piece off and chew it, getting the sweet juice out. The juice was very sweet and lots of times it would be enjoyed this way. Of course the real reason we grew sugar cane was to make syrup.

At the cane mill, all of us would gather because it was syrup making time which meant it was a group effort. We started the process by squeezing all the juice out of the cane. We did this with a cane mill, which consisted of three vertical steel wheels about eight inches tall that were real close to each other. Gears were attached to the top in such a way so that two wheels were pulling the cane in and the other was pushing it out. A long pole was attached to the top that stuck out about fifteen feet and a mule was hooked up to the pole and made to walk in a circle around the cane mill causing the system to work. When the cane was fed in between the three wheels the juice would come gushing out, running down into a pan attached at the bottom of the mill. There was an opening on one side where a bucket hung with a piece of cheese cloth stretched over the top to let only the juice into the bucket. The long stalks of cane that came out of the other side were referred to as guts.

The collected juice was heated to make it into syrup. To do this, Mom and Dad used a pan that was about two feet wide, four feet long and six inches deep with handles on either side that ran the full length. The pan sat on top of a brick firebox with a chimney at one end for the smoke to come out of with the other end open so they could keep adding wood to maintain the right amount of heat. The juice was put into the pan, placed on the firebox to heat and when it came to a slow simmer, wood was added or removed to keep the heat just right so the juice would not burn or scorch. As the juice simmered for a while, Mom would scoop some out with a spoon and put it in a saucer, then wave it in the air to cool it off. As it cooled, if it had been cooked long enough, it would thicken into syrup. If you cooked it too long or got it too hot, the syrup would be real dark and be a little strong in taste. When the syrup was just right, they would lift the pan with all the syrup and sit it off to the side to cool. After it had cooled it was poured into jars and tops were put on. The syrup they made was golden in color and real sweet. The people in the area thought Mom and Dad made the best syrup. This syrup was used in many ways to sweeten things such as tea or coffee, and on pancakes, biscuits and cakes.

If you would leave syrup in a jar for a long period of time, the syrup would form little lumps of hard candy called rock candy. We really didn't have candy from a store back then; rock candy was the kind of candy we had. We did sometimes have chewing gum but it came from a tree and interestingly enough the tree was called a sweet gum tree. We would cut a notch in the bark of the gum tree and the juice would run out of the tree and then harden. We would take a piece of this and chew it like people today would do chewing gum.

Learning to plow the front field. Before I tell you about plowing the fields, keep in mind I was only around eight years old at the time. Back in those days we didn't have a tractor. We did the plowing of the fields with a mule pulling what we called a single turn plow. This kind of plowing was used to break up the dirt in the field to get it ready to plant and in the springtime the field would be plowed again before planting. A single turn plow is a plow that throws the dirt in one direction. It has handles coming up from the plow and you have to hold the handles in the upright position. Tilting the handles up in the air made the plow go deeper and if you pushed down on the handles the plow would come up so you had to constantly keep the handles level. If you were just plowing away and you stuck the point in the ground too far, it would be more than a mule could pull. Then you'd have to pull the plow backwards to get the point out of the ground and tilt it up so the mule could go again. I was so small that if I had gotten the plow down in the ground too deep, I would never have been able to pull it back to get it loose so I had to be real careful as I was plowing the field.

When my Daddy and older brother got to the end of the field they would just turn the mule around and pick up the plow and flip the plow around ready to go back in the other direction, but I couldn't do that. I had to walk the mule out at the end of the field, lay the plow down on its side so it wouldn't get stuck in the ground, then walk the mule in a circle dragging the plow till I got back to where I was to start again. Anyway, when I was plowing the front field and felt tired I remember I would stop and sit down and rest for a while. I don't think I ever got the field completed but I did some plowing and that was the important thing. It's hard to believe that I could get out there and do that because I was so young and such a little fellow, but if I wanted to do something I sure would try. I have always been that way, no matter what you put in front of me I would try and figure out how to get it done.

A single turn plow

The single turn plow could be made into a double plow by adding a blade to the other side. It was used to cut a trench or furrow where seed could be planted and covered by another piece of equipment that scratched a groove, dropped the seed, and a V-shaped wheel would squeeze dirt over the seeds. This planter sure beat dropping the seed and covering it by hand like we used to do with a hoe.

Church, Hunting & Fishing

Most Sundays we took the mule and wagon and went off to the Pentecostal Holiness church about three miles away. It was a small church and as I recall there was no Sunday school rooms or Sunday school classes, only preaching as we called it. The community cemetery was at another church, a Methodist church about half way between our house and the Pentecostal church we attended.

One particular Sunday morning in the summer, Dad stopped the wagon in the middle of the bridge over Mungdam Creek, stripped off his clothes and dove in the dark swirling water. He took a swim around, climbed out, put his clothes back on and went on to church. You see, back then there were very few cars around because most people traveled by wagon. The road was dirt and you may not see another soul all day, especially on Sunday.

Once we got to church, most of the men were standing under the big oak tree smoking or cleaning their fingernails from the week's work, but Mom would take all of us inside to take a seat. This church believed in shouting, speaking in tongues, amen's and halleluiah, and a lot of jumping around as the sprit moved people. This seemed to be controlled to a point because there was a certain time during the service when the shouting would start and then would be calmed down by starting a song, then the service would be brought to a close. During all of this, I usually made my way to the back of the church.

One particular night, I think a Sunday or one night during a revival, I was sitting in the back with a friend playing, paying no attention to what was going on. All of a sudden this lady came to us and tried to get us to come down to the altar and confess our sins and be saved. Well, this scared me because I didn't want to go down there in front of all those people. This experience affected me and my view of religion for the rest of my life. To this day I cannot stand to be in a service of this type and even the raising of hands disturbs me.

My feelings towards God are one of quiet respect and humility and emotional outbursts bother me. I do remember when my Dad accepted Christ. He was at the altar during a service and got up and threw his cigarettes out the window. You see, back then almost everything was a sin, including smoking, based on how you interpreted the Bible.

Mom would have the preacher over for Sunday dinner sometimes because back then, someone would always invite the preacher over to eat. She would usually kill a chicken by going out in the yard, picking one out, running it down, catching it, chopping its head off, then cleaning and cooking it. This one chicken had to feed everyone in the family and since there were eight of us plus the preacher, one piece of chicken per person was all you got. I remember when I was older and out on my own being able to have more than one piece of chicken. What a treat.

When I was about six or seven we were coming home from church one Sunday night in our old car and I was looking out the window at the stars. Suddenly I saw a five in the sky as plain as could be and I exclaimed to everyone "Look at the five!" but they could not see it. I now know I must have been seeing stars lined up that looked like a five to me, but since then I have always considered five to be my lucky number. Even when I got older the number five continued to play a part in my life. I have always been interested in looking up at the heavens, even as a young boy. Living where we did at night it got dark, really dark, and I would look up at the moon and stars and wonder about it all. By the time I was ten I was talking about man going to the moon someday. I'll talk more about that later.

Hunting rats and fishing in the pond were two of the things we did for fun. For example we would go down to the barn and kill rats, and I don't mean mice, I mean big old rats. In the barn we kept corn piled up in one corner and the rats would naturally come in to eat the corn. Well, in the winter some of the rats would crawl up to the top of the barn above the crack where the two pieces of tin roof meet, and lie in the hollow between that crack and the half-circle piece of tin above that kept the rain out. The rats would lie in this hollow because it was warm but the only way to get out was at the two ends. So we would sneak up there and stick an ear of corn in both ends so the rats couldn't get out, then we would take sharp sticks and poke up through the crack and kill them. Afterwards, we would take the corn out and slide the rats to the end and let them drop to the ground. Our Daddy liked for us to do this because the rats ate up a lot of stuff.

We didn't have any toys to play with way down there in the country so we made our own toys out of whatever we had. Like the time me and my two brothers went out to a pond that was in the woods near our house. It wasn't much of a pond, probably only two feet deep and not very big but we got lucky and found a couple of old crossties that our Daddy had cut and shaped by hand that had not been picked up by the timber truck yet. What we did was took those crossties, nailed some boards across and made ourselves a raft. After we built the raft we would take fishing line and tie it onto a small limb and float out in the pond and catch little small fish. Nobody ever fell in and of course we never caught a fish big enough to take home to our Mama, but we had many happy times on that raft.

The men usually hunted with dogs. They would split up in the woods and each person would go to a place where they knew the deer would usually run to. The man with the dogs would turn them loose and try to get the dogs moving towards the other men, hoping they would get a shot. We had a hunting dog too. He was a great big deer hound and solid black. We called him Snowball.

When the grownups went hunting and got a deer, they would come home, skin the deer, and cut up the meat. Then they would separate the meat in as many piles as there were hunters. One fellow would put his hand on a pile of meat and another fellow with his back turned would call out the name of one of the hunters and that pile of meat went to whoever's name he called. They did that until everyone had a portion. The man who killed the deer would get the skin and antlers along with his meat. Everyone who was involved got a share.

Hogs ran free in the woods and putting food out for them kept them sort of tame and was referred to as free range hogs. Some of the hogs would get wild though from being in the woods so much. When Daddy would see some of the wild ones around he would get Fido and go in the woods after them. He would put Fido on their trail and pretty soon Fido would get one cornered. When Daddy caught up with Fido and the hog, Fido would lunge in and grab the hog by the ear and stay right beside the hog, turning every time the hog would turn. These hogs had long tusks from living in the woods and rooting to get things to eat but by standing next to the hog, the hog could not reach Fido with its tusks.

After Fido had the hog worn down some, Daddy would sneak in from behind and grab the hogs' two hind feet and pick his back end up off the ground. The hog couldn't do much then with just his front feet. Daddy would tie him up and take him back to the farm with the mule and put him in a pen. If it was a boar, which is a male hog, Daddy would castrate him or cut his testicles out, or as we said on the farm "cut his nuts out." If you didn't do this, the meat would not taste very good. After the boar was castrated we had to keep him for several months but usually until fall when it turned cold. That was hog killing time and he would be added to the list.

There was this one time when Daddy went out after some wild hogs with my brother Lester. Fido was rushing around looking for hogs when one big one came out of the bushes and went straight at Dad. Dad said he got set and was going to kick the hog in the snoot but when he kicked the hog swung his head up and his tusk caught in Daddy's pants leg and ripped it open all the way to the pockets, barely missing his skin. Lester thought the hog had hurt Daddy but the only thing it did was rip his pants and cause him to fall down. Lucky for him the hog kept going because if the hog had stopped, Daddy would have been in a heap of trouble. Right after that happened, Dad told Lester to go home and get the shotgun. When Lester returned with the gun they trailed the hog and killed it. Life was a real struggle back then.

Mungdam Creek was mentioned earlier. This was the creek out behind our house on the other side of the field and a place we caught a lot of fish. Our Dad made a fish trap out of small wire and shaped into a square box about thirty inches square. On one side it had a hole shaped like a funnel made in the wire that extended inside the trap. The fish could swim in through the hole and would come out into the middle of the box. Of course, when they tried to get out through the wire they always tried to get out around the edges and never seemed to be able to figure out how to go back to the middle to get back out through that small hole.

The trap was always set with the opening downstream so fish swimming upstream would enter into the trap and then could not get out. Daddy also had wings made from the same wire on each side of this trap that extended over to the banks of the stream, basically cutting off the entire creek. The purpose of the wings on either side was to force the fish into the middle to find an opening to go upstream. So when we needed fresh fish we would just go back to the creek, pull the trap out of the creek, and take out what we needed. Pulling the trap out also meant somebody had to get into the dark water of that creek, usually one of us boys. Even though we did not know how to swim, we would crawl in the water and pull it out anyway. The trap had an opening in the top covered with wire so we could swing it open and reach down in the trap and take out however many fish we needed. What we didn't need we left in the trap and put it back in the creek. They would be there the next time we needed some more fish. This way we always had a fresh source of food. This was not done for fun; it was all done because we needed something to eat. Folks back then knew how to live off the land.

One day in late summer, my older brother Lester and I went squirrel hunting. A beautiful orange sun was just coming up on the horizon when Lester said, "If you want to go squirrel hunting, come on with me Sam." Well I was out of that bed faster than you could whistle. We grabbed a couple of baked sweet potatoes, a cold biscuit and some cracklings and out the back door we went. I was a scrawny little kid but I had learned to do about anything I wanted to. On this day I wanted to go with my older brother Lester squirrel hunting in the swamp. You see, back then when we went hunting it wasn't for sport, it was to get something to eat.

Dad kept lots of honey bees in the back of the house so to get to the swamp we first had to go around the bee boxes and to the side of the field behind the house. In that area, there were two fields separated by a path. When we got to the back side of these fields we climbed over the fence and right there was where the swamp started. This swamp covered several thousand acres. If you look at a South Carolina map you'll see that it is located northwest of Charleston, South Carolina and known as Hellhole Swamp. Now, this swamp was not necessarily always covered with water. It was during the rainy season but at other times it had some places where it was wet and other parts that were dry. The water wasn't muddy either; it was black looking like real strong tea. Somebody said it was the tannin from the leaves and the trees and stuff that caused the water to be real dark. Anyway, there wasn't much vegetation on the ground, nor were there many small bushes. The trees were mostly cypress, oak and hickory and there was always moss hanging from the branches. With such a leafy canopy the sunlight was all but blocked out.

As we walked into the swamp looking for squirrels, my brother spotted something up a tree and he motioned for me to go around to the other side of the tree and shake a bush. I remembered my Daddy saying he saw black panthers in this swamp sometimes when he had been hunting, but this wasn't a black panther, it was a squirrel. Now, when you are hunting squirrels and you walk into the woods, the squirrels hide from you. You need to have two people so one person can stand still while the other one walks around the other side of the tree. The squirrel will move around the tree away from the one that just walked around. When the squirrel does that, the person that's got the rifle and doing the hunting would draw a bead on the squirrel and "bang."

On this particular day, my job was to just walk around the other side of the trees to scare squirrels so Lester could do the shooting. I was not allowed to shoot because back then there wasn't much money to buy bullets and every bullet had to bring home a squirrel. One time my brother missed and he got so nervous he had to sit and calm down before going on with the hunting. After the squirrel was shot and killed, it was also my job to pick him up. When I went to pick up the squirrel, I was real careful because sometimes people had been bitten by squirrels that were still alive. There's this story about a fellow who got bit like that, plumb through the thumb. They had to pry the squirrel's mouth open just to get his thumb loose. Boy, I bet that hurt. Well, I wasn't going to let that happen, and even though I was only seven I still knew to be careful. So, I picked up a stick and poked the squirrel to see if he would move. This was a sure way to tell if an animal was dead. He didn't move so I picked him up and looped a leather strap around his head to carry him with, then ran to catch up with my brother who was already looking for another squirrel.

A little further on in the woods we came to Mungdam Creek and headed to the part of the creek where we usually crossed. That area was about eight to ten feet wide with a big old tree that had fallen across the creek and that's where we would always cross over to the other side. On this particular day however, the water was real high because of the recent rains and was running over the log and moving real fast. Lester walked on across, and being bigger and heavier he had no problem. When I started across, the swift water threw me off balance and I fell right into the dark water. I did not know how to swim so I was grabbing at tree limbs as I was being washed down the creek. I managed to grab some, but the force of the water pushing me would break the limb. Lester was running along the edge of the bank hollering for me to grab onto something and just about that time I saw a big limb that was hanging out over the water and grabbed it. The water washed me around towards the bank and the limb did not break. Lester was hollering for me to hang on and then waded out in the water and pulled me to safety. You know what we did? We just went right on hunting. Falling in the creek was just another part of life growing up in the country.

Hog Killing Time

In the fall of the year after it had turned cold, the family would all get together for hog killing time. Hog killing always happened in the fall of the year because it was easier to process the meat once it had gotten colder. The hogs were usually shot with a 22 rifle in the head and their throat was cut so that most of the blood would drain out. After that, they would put the hog down in a barrel full of hot water.

The barrel was placed in a shallow hole in the ground where a fire had been built so the water would boil. They would then put the hog in and turn it around so that all areas on one end had been covered with the hot water. Once one end was done, the hog was pulled out and turned around so they could do the other end. The hot water caused the hair on the hog to come out and all of this was done before the hog had its innards taken out. After the hog had been scalded with the hot water, they would pull it out of the barrel and lay it on boards on the ground, scraping off all of the hair with a flat piece of metal that was sharp on one edge. The hair came off real easy but boy did it smell bad. You know how a dog smells when he gets wet, well this was worse, a lot worse. After cleaning the hair off, they would hang the hog up on a pole that was fastened to two posts in the ground that was braced real good. This pole had to be real strong because some of the hogs would weigh three hundred pounds, and it would take three or more people to get the hog hung on the pole. The rear legs were cut so a steel hook could be stuck through between the leg and the tendons. These tendons are real strong and can hold all the weight of the hog.

When they took the intestines out, they would save the small intestines for making sausage. These were cleaned real good and then scraped inside and out. When they were through, all that was left was a real thin clear membrane, kind of like a long balloon that you couldn't quite see through. These were put in water to keep then soft until they were ready to stuff with the sausage meat. You know those little link sausages that you love so much with breakfast, well guess what that meat is packed in, you guessed it, little innards. I think now they use a man made thing, but they were referred to as casings back in the old days.

The hog was then cut into small portions, the hams the shoulders, pork chops and fat back. The liver was also used. The meat was all cured either with salt or with smoke. This was done in a smoke house. The smoke house was a small building, about ten by twelve feet, with a shelf running around the end and two sides. The building was sealed up tight to keep the flies from getting in, with only a small screened opening high on one end for smoke to get out. This opening had a piece of cloth over it that came from a flour sack. In those days, flour and other store purchased bag items were in pretty cloth bags. Sometimes these cloth bags were also used to make clothes.

The meat that was not cured whole was ground up in a hand cranked meat grinder and all kinds of spices were added that gave the meat a special flavor. All this was mixed into the meat by hand. You would literally take your hands and squish the ground up meat until all the flavoring was mixed in real good. To make the sausage, the intestine was pushed over an opening of the meat grinder and held in place while someone ran the flavored meat back through the grinder again. The ground meat would come out the hole and into the intestine and slide all the way through until it was full. After both ends were tied off, the long sausage was then twisted in short sections to create sausage links. These links were hung in the smoke house and smoked. Other meat such as hams and shoulders were spread out on a shelf in the smoke house and covered in salt. Each day they would check it, turn it over and make sure it stayed covered with salt. Over time, the salt would penetrate the meat and cure it. While they were doing the cutting up of the meat, the hog's brains would be taken out and scrambled with eggs. This was always a special treat.

The hog's belly, the skin and the fat, would be cut into large pieces. Cuts were made in the fat side all the way down to the skin in a checker board pattern and then it was put in a big black wash pot with a fire lit under it. This was actually the same pot Mom used to boil her clothes in on wash day. As the pot got hot, the grease would cook out of the fat and after the skin and fat had cooked down, it would come to the top of the grease. Once it was done, it was taken out and drained, broken into small pieces and stored in a large can. This skin was called cracklings and eaten like you would eat meat skins. All of the grease would be poured into a large can and stored as lard to be used for cooking. Today, you can by lard at the grocery store because some people still cook with it. It has a very good flavor. Once the hams and shoulders were cured, string was tied around the leg end and hung on nails in the rafters of the smoke house. When we wanted some meat we would go out, get a ham down and cut some off of it. We always soaked it in water first to get some of the salty brine out and then we would fry it. This type of meat is still eaten today; it is called country ham.

Hogs and God - a story told by my brother Lester when he was about sixteen years old.

Daddy had been doing roadwork on the W.P.A. and had saved enough money to buy a Hampshire hog that was ready to have piglets. He was planning to breed some of them when they were grown so he could continue to have Hampshire hogs each year. So, Daddy bought the hog and put her in a pen down by the barn. After the piglets were born, Daddy told Lester to stay away from the pen for a while because the hog would spook easily and she might step on a piglet and kill it. You see back then, all those pigs represented meat later on. Lester stayed away as he was told but his younger sister kept pestering him to go see the piglets. Finally, he agreed and took her down to the pen and sure enough, the hog got spooked and stepped on one of the piglets and killed it. Daddy found out what happened.

Lester said that Daddy beat him with the yard broom until blood was running down his back. Afterward, Lester said he ran around behind the house and started praying saying to God, "If you are real and agree that Daddy should not have beat me like he did, then let all the piglets die one by one." Lester said the next day one piglet was found dead, and the next day after that another piglet was found dead. After the third piglet had died Daddy could not figure out what was going on and said as much. Finally, Lester spoke up and told Daddy what he had prayed for. Lester said Daddy just stood there looking at him, not knowing what to say. Later when our Grand-Dad (Daddy's daddy) heard about it he told our Daddy to never lay a hand on Lester again. Maybe he said that because he felt Daddy had done wrong, or maybe it was concern that Lester may pray down something even worse to happen if he got a beating like that again. Whatever the reason, Lester said Daddy never whipped him again.

School & Trouble I Got Into

Our school consisted of four classrooms and an auditorium. There was a large central entrance way with two classrooms on the left and two classrooms on the right. The auditorium was centered behind the entrance way. Above the entrance way there was a bell tower with a rope hanging down so we could ring the bell to call everyone in for classes. We studied the basic things like reading, writing and math but we also had to learn the books of the Bible. We were even made to stand in the auditorium and recite it in front of the whole class. I stumbled on a few but made it through okay.

Most kids today are out for the summer in August but we were always in school. I guess because we were all farm kids the school year was set up differently so we could be home to help our families for planting and harvesting. I was almost nine years old, and can remember being in school when World War II ended. The date was August 14, 1945. A few days before, the United States had dropped two atomic bombs on Japan and they had finally surrendered. Our teacher had heard the news on the radio and told me and another boy to go ring the bell. We were so small that after we pulled the rope down, on the way back up it would lift us off the floor. We rang the bell for a very long time. That was a happy day for the world.

The one thing I did that I am most ashamed of was when Alton Fort and I schemed to stop the bus from making it to school. Now Alton was two years older than I was, so that put him about ten and me about eight. He and I figured that if we put sand in the gas tank it would make it stop. Now, we must have heard this from some adult because I don't think two seven or eight year olds could come up with that all by themselves. Well, we plotted what we were going to do and one day when the bus was stopped at the Post Office, one of us got the school bus driver Mr. Patz's attention while the other went around and put a handful of sand in the tank. I think it was a day or two later on the way to school, about half way between Uncle Ezra's and Aunt Virginia's store, when the bus stopped. We spent quite a while there before help arrived. Later at school, the teacher found out about what we had done because Alton's brother Ray had told on us. Alton and I got our tails whipped but good by the teacher too. They did that back then and I learned a very good lesson that day.

Like I said, if I didn't do what I was told to do or got into trouble, I got my butt whipped, and not always by Mom or Dad. At one point, my brother Lester being the oldest had to run the farm when Daddy was sick with asthma. If he told me to do something and I didn't do it, he whipped my butt. One time Mom sent me down to the barn to feed the chickens. Well, I ending up getting sidetracked and forgot. When I wandered back up to the house and she found out I had not fed the chickens she took the yard broom and beat me real good. I remember being on the ground with her flailing me good with the broom.

My curiosity about how things worked sometimes got me in trouble too. Like the time when we lived on the farm I took Mom's one and only wind up clock and took it apart to see how it worked. Just as I had it opened up, Mom walked in and took a hard look at me and said "When I come back in here you better have it back together and it better work." I did and she was very happy. Another time in Rock Hill, South Carolina I do remember Daddy whipping me about something. It happened in the kitchen and although the back door was open, the screen door was closed. When he finished up whipping me, he put his foot against my butt and shoved me so hard out the door that I landed on the ground and never touched the steps. It's a good thing too because those steps were made of stacked concrete blocks.

Today people will say, Oh! I was abused as a child and that made me do this or that! Baloney. The truth is with all that happened, even though at the time I was mad for being punished, I have no ill feeling about it today. It was just the way it was and a part of growing up. I am the person I am today because of my upbringing and the lessons learned during those times. I had, and have, great love for my Mother and Father and I am very thankful for the way I was raised.

Christmas at Our House

When I was growing up in Shulerville we celebrated Christmas as Christ's birthday, but gifts and Christmas trees~~well, there is not much to remember. In fact it wasn't until I was ten years old that I can remember having a tree or decorations or anything like that. You must realize that I was born in 1936 towards the end of the Great Depression on a farm, and with a brother and two sisters older than me. We had very little and made do with what we had so Christmas presents were rare. However, I do remember looking forward to going over to my Aunt and Uncles house. They were well off compared to most folks in Hellhole Swamp.

I remember one year my Aunt gave me a small glass container that looked like some animal with a lid. It had small pieces of candy in it and I didn't have to share. The only gift I remember getting at home was a plastic harmonica that we called a mouth organ. I was about five or six years old and can remember looking through the Sears and Roebuck catalog and dreaming of having that little mouth organ. My Mom ended up ordering it that year and I got it for Christmas. I played it, or tried to play it, until the corners of my mouth were so raw my Mom took it from me for a while so my mouth could heal. Through my tenth birthday those are the only two gifts that I can recall getting for Christmas. We moved from the farm in 1946 to Rock Hill, South Carolina and Christmas's got better after that. The thing is, Christmas is not about how much you get, it's about love and we had plenty of that.

My Brother Ran the Farm

My older brother Lester ran the farm because Daddy had a disease called bronchial asthma. Most people today just call it asthma and it causes you to have trouble breathing. He had always had asthma but it became worse as he got older. Daddy spent many a night sitting up in a chair gasping for breath and during the spring of the year it was worse than other times. With all the trees, bushes and grass growing, there was a lot of pollen during that time of the year. Daddy tried to farm as best he could but with Lester being the oldest child he had to take on more and more of the daily chores. By the time I was eight years old, Lester was sixteen and did most of the work. Running the farm was more difficult at certain times of the year too. In the early spring, the fields had to be planted and in the fall harvesting took place. Those times of the year also happened to be when our Father was having his worst time with asthma.

When Daddy was doing carpentry work or at the Navy Yard in Charleston, he left Lester in charge. Running the farm caused my brother to take on great responsibility before he was really ready for it. He would tell the rest of us what to do and if we did not do it, we got our butt's beat. Lester even stayed out of school to take care of the farm and only went through the ninth grade. I think Lester really hated that he wasn't able to attend school and held this against our Father, although it was not our Dad's fault.

Leaving the Farm Behind

One summer while Lester was running the farm, Dad worked for a contractor helping to build a bridge across the Santee River near Jamestown, South Carolina. I worked there too one summer as a water boy when I was about nine years old. In those days we did not have all the rules about how old you had to be to work. As the water boy, I would carry an open bucket of water with a metal dipper around to the men working and they would use the dipper to get a drink, then I would take it to the next person. This would go on until all the water was gone. Everybody used the same dipper time after time. I would then go fill the bucket again and make the same rounds. I would do this all day long.

Anyway, when the Santee River bridge project in Jamestown was finally completed, the contractor told everybody he had another contract to build a textile plant called "Celanese" in Rock Hill, South Carolina. When he asked all the men to come to Rock Hill to work on this next job, a number of them decided to go, including my Dad. They all stayed in a concrete block building with army cots lined up from one end to the other. There were toilets and showers at the back end and a big coal heater in front of the toilets so it was able to heat the whole space (see the picture on the next page).

Things went along real good that first week. So good in fact that about the middle of the second week Daddy wrote my Momma a letter (he could not call because we didn't have any telephones back then) and told her he was doing so well with his asthma that we were going to move. Notice he didn't ask her if she wanted to move, he just said "we are moving." Maybe he did it that way because he had been sick for so long and when he found out about the job in Rock Hill he and Momma had already discussed the possibility of moving. A Doctor had told him once he would do better with his asthma if he lived up towards the mountains. Rock Hill was not in the mountains, but the altitude there was much higher.

The bunk house - 2012

Well, when my Mama got the letter it basically said we're moving, pack up everything and I will be there with a truck on Saturday. So, that Saturday Daddy showed up with a stake bodied truck (that's an open truck with wood rails along the side and back) and we loaded our few meager possessions in the back and tied it down so nothing would fall off. The rest of us followed in the pickup truck. The pickup had a shell over the back so me and my two brothers Furman and Mendel ("Tibby" and "M.L.") got in the back with the oldest brother Lester driving. My two sisters Evie and Alma rode up front with Lester while Momma and Daddy drove the stake bodied truck with all of our stuff in it.

Early Sunday morning we lit out for Rock Hill, South Carolina for a new beginning and a different life than what we were used to. I was ten years old when we moved and although it was quite an adventure, I thank God it happened. I have often wondered what would have become of me and my brothers and sisters if we had stayed on the farm. Rock Hill offered the whole family new opportunities.

Moving to Rock Hill, South Carolina

It was October or November of 1946 and we got there late on a Sunday afternoon. When we saw our new home, the place was a plywood building from the war. There were three spaces in an L shape and no inner walls that designated rooms. The outer walls were wood studs covered by half inch plywood and no insulation at all. Wood joists supported the roof and hanging from the joists were three light bulbs, one in each of the three spaces.

There was no such thing as a bathroom, although we were used to that. I think there was an outhouse but I really don't remember. For water there was a community faucet down on the next road. We used a large glass jug that held three or four gallons of water with a wire handle and a wooden piece in the middle of the wire to carry it with. We would collect water in the jug and two of us would carry it home. The only heat in the house was a coal heater in the middle of the place. I do not remember what we cooked on unless it was the big heater. The few pieces of furniture we brought from Shulerville were set up so we had a place to sleep. Of course, Daddy went to work right away so he would have money coming in to see us through the winter.

I remember one time it was freezing cold and my Dad was bringing home a load of coal in the pickup truck. Before he got to the house, the truck got stuck in a mud hole and could not get out. We had to bring the coal to the house in buckets and the truck stayed there until Dad could get someone to help him get it out. We suffered through the winter in this shack and I do not remember school that whole winter. All I remember is bringing coal, going to get water, and trying to stay warm.

Daddy was only renting this place though. He had bought some property back out near highway 21 on Williams Street with plans to build a house in the spring. All through the winter on weekends, when the weather would permit, we "the family" would work on the new house. We did all the work on the house ourselves. The foundation, plumbing, electrical, sheetrock, etc., we did everything. The only thing Dad paid for was the septic tank and maybe digging the hole for the tank. The outside walls were covered with wooden boards and must have been boards from a gum tree because they were so hard you could barely get a nail through them. The latest thing for covering the outside was asbestos shingles about twelve by twenty-four in size. Lots of new houses were using asbestos but the shingles were very hard to nail. In order to nail them to the wall we had to use a special tool that would first punch a hole for the nail. That was the only way to get them up on the wall.

The new house was not fancy, just a simple plan. It had three bedrooms and a bath down one side, and a living room, dining room and kitchen down the other side with a door on either end. It also had a stairway going up to the attic so cots could be set up down each side for people to sleep. In the spring of 1947 we moved in and it sure was nice to have our own place. Mom and Dad slept in one bedroom, my two sisters in the second bedroom, and my older brother in the third bedroom. My two younger brothers and I were in the attic space that had been finished. It had a window at both ends which we used sometimes on the weekend to sneak out of and hang out with other kids in the neighborhood.

I think I have already said that Mom and Dad went to bed at dark and we had to do likewise. They wanted everything quiet but I wanted to listen to some shows on the radio like the Lone Ranger and others. I was always tinkering with things and had learned how to disconnect one of the speaker wires in the back of the radio so I could clip on an old crystal radio headset I got from somewhere and listen in. I was always interested in radio and electronics and this would move me in different directions as I got older. When the show went off I would take the clips off the wires and hook the one I had cut back up so the radio would work again when my Mom turned it on. I never did get caught.

We lived in the house on Williams Street for many years and this is where I grew up. This is also where I learned to make money by selling newspapers, ointment, razor blades and anything else I could get my hands on that I thought I could make a little money with.

All of this was right after World War II and a lot of people were looking for work. While Dad continued to do carpentry work helping to build the new Celanese plant, many of Dad's friends from Shulerville came to Rock Hill to find work. Some of these people stayed in the same concrete block building where my Dad had stayed when he first came to Rock Hill. All of these people were looking for a cheap place to stay and some asked my Dad if they could room and board at our house. Our Mom and Dad said yes and began to take people in. Daddy bought army cots and set them up in the attic, one behind the other, down both walls. We only had one bathroom but these were working men and didn't spend much time at our house so we survived. Mom would fix breakfast and prepare lunches, but I don't think she cooked supper for them. My Dad was working full time like the other men, but I remember him helping with breakfast and fixing lunches. I don't remember what Mom and Dad charged for the men to board there but the money was really good.

At one point Mom and Dad had so many boarders they had them sleeping on the floor in the living room as well as in the attic. My two younger brothers and I had moved downstairs into the bedroom where our older brother had been sleeping, so the boarders could have the attic. Lester (the oldest) had already moved out into a trailer behind the house with the girl he had married, her name was Gerry, so this made room for everyone we had staying at the house. We had boarders at the house through that first summer and into the next year as I recall. In the meantime, those of us that were in school had already started.

This is the house on Williams Street that we built.

Left to Right: Me, Furman, and Mendel standing in our front yard. I was about 11 years old.

Grammar School in Rock Hill

I had made friends with the kids across the street; their last name was Chidister. The boy's name was Eddie and I think he had two sisters and a younger brother. I went to school with Eddie at the Red River School which was north of where we lived. The school was located in a cotton mill village on Red River Road. As you came into the village on the main road, you took a right at the cotton mill and then would travel up along a winding road to the top of a hill. On top of the hill sat the school and a small chapel.

The school in Red River wasn't much and I don't remember learning a whole lot there except how to fight. There was one kid there who was the bully and always gave Eddie a hard time. I remember the very first day of school, this kid, I think his name was Earl Johnson, came up and spit in Eddie's face. It made me so mad and I asked Eddie why he didn't do something about it. That's when I realized that Earl and his friends ruled the playground. I wasn't going to have that so over the next few days and weeks I began to gather around me the kids that were being bullied and we formed our own group.

Pretty soon it reached a point where Earl and I ended up in a big fight rolling all over the red dirt on the school ground. I remember I had finally gotten on top when Earl's sister, Gladys, who was I don't know how old, but big, came over and pulled me off. The fight was over when the bell rang and we headed back into the classroom. After I sat down, Gladys came in and slapped me so hard I thought I was going to pass out. Later, after we had moved on to another school, we heard this kid Earl had burned the school down.

Sometimes the other group would single out some of those in our group. I remember one day after recess looking for one of the boys but we couldn't find him. Several of us went into the woods looking, because we played back in the woods a lot, and found him tied to a tree. The other group had done this to him and had left him there. There was always a controversy going on between us and that other group.

Sometimes we'd go out for recess and go in the woods and play and not come back until it was time to go home. We would climb small pine trees, saplings we called them, and swing the tree until it bent over a bit then grab the next one and swing from tree to tree. When we were ready to stop, we would simply grab one and swing out really hard and when the tree was bent over far enough we would drop off to the ground. We had lots of fun but we didn't learn very much and this hindered me later in life as I entered middle and high school.

The next school I went to was Ebenezer Avenue. It was a junior high or middle school as they call it today. I remember getting into a fight the first day of school and a lot of the kids there were bigger. You see, when I was a little fellow growing up on the farm I didn't take any crap from anybody. If someone tried to push me around, they had a fight on their hands and that followed me all the way through middle school. For some reason though, when I entered high school this changed and I think it might have been because the kids in high school were so much bigger. Plus, I was picked on by the other bigger kids and was not a part of what was going on in high school. I will talk more about that later on.

Ebenezer Avenue

Life on Williams Street

Living in our new house on Williams Street was really nice compared to the shack we moved into before winter. We had indoor plumbing and our own individual bedrooms, even though we shared them with our sisters or brothers. We still had chores though and certain things we had to do to help out around the house. Williams Street was located on the north side of Rock Hill just off highway 21. One block over was Cedar Grove Lane. These two streets were connected by cross streets and one was named Lewis Street after my Dad. All the kids in the two street areas would hang out walking or riding bicycles. There was nowhere else to go, except out on highway 21 and that was dangerous. Most of our time growing up was spent in this area.

My two younger brothers Furman and Mendel were about two years apart in age and we spent a lot of our time playing in the woods. We would always start by building a fort, a camp, or a tree house to play in. These were usually made of whatever available material we could put our hands on. I remember one fort was built of stone, another of small trees and limbs, and one was beside a creek where a large patch of sugar cane was growing. To build this last one we started at the edge of the creek and cut a path into the center of the cane patch. There we cleared out a square area, took the canes we had cut and constructed a fort by weaving them in and out of the cane we had left growing which made it a very good enclosure. There was one thing all these forts had in common though; we never finished any of them. We would always move on to some other adventure.

We would venture all over the country side, miles away from home, delighted in finding and exploring new and exciting spots. This time of growing up was around 1950 and we did not have much to play with except what we could dream up. I remember the swimming hole we made on a creek by piling rocks across the stream and causing the water to back up deep enough for us to play in. One time we found this terraced hill so we named it Lewis Mountain and another time we found a big hole in the ground where quartz rock was all over the place so we figured someone was looking for gold. Sometimes we would even ride our bicycles out to the dam on the Catawba River.

My bike was fixed up with parts I had scrounged around and found and all painted like it was new. I also had a tool box that I made and had attached to the rear frame of my bike. I took a long Spam can and expanded the top part so it would fit over the bottom part and attached it to the frame. It fit tight and was water proof and I kept several tools in it as well as patch material for the inner tubes in case I had a flat. I remember one time some kid put a tomato in the can and one day I went in it for some reason and it was a mess. I tried to find out who did it because I was going to kick his butt, but I never did.

The lake behind the dam on the Catawba River was called Lake Wylie. There we would go swimming. Other times we would ride all the way to Red River Road, down past the cotton mill and along the railroad tracks to the river. We would leave the bicycles and walk across the bridge, but not on top where the train runs, oh no. We would go under the tracks where two boards had been laid down side-by-side on the steel framing, and some of those boards were old and broken.

We would make our way to the other side where an island was near the other bank. There was a tall tree next to the bridge that someone had tied with a rope and hooked to the bridge. We would pull the top of the tree over to the edge of the bridge, then grab the top of the tree and swing off, climbing down to the island so we could explore the area. The top of that tree wasn't very large and if it had broken we would have fallen thirty feet to the rocks below. What was fascinating about this island was it was known as Goat Island. I never saw a goat or any sign of a goat though but that didn't matter, it was always an adventure. One time, when we returned to where we had left our bicycles, some of the local kids had thrown them down the bank of the railroad track. Other times were spent hanging out in our neighborhood just playing and riding our bicycles with the other kids.

After we had been living on Williams Street for a while, a drive-in movie theater was built just over from Cedar Grove Lane. It was called The Auto Drive-In. There was another one on the other side of town called The Fort Rock Drive-In; a combination of the name of the town Rock Hill and a nearby town called Fort Mill. During the summer, the neighborhood kids would gather beside the fence and watch the movies on Friday or Saturday night. We couldn't hear very well so someone would slip under or over the chain link fence and turn up all the speakers along our side of the parking area. Sometimes the manager would come out and turn them all down but as soon as he would leave we would turn them up again. Up where Cedar Grove Lane met highway 21 was Snipe's Upholstery Shop with junk chairs and sofas out back. We began to bring some of these over to the fence so we would have a nice place to sit and watch the movie. We had some grand old times there on the weekends watching free movies. We also took advantage when our neighbors got a new TV. It was sometime around 1952 and some of us kids would sneak over at night, sit on their front porch and watch whatever was on. We finally got a our own TV several years later. You know, back then you could only get like three channels and the TV went off the air at midnight.

One time there was a large group at the drive-in watching movies and the three Finley brothers started to pick on another boy. This boy would not fight so I spoke up and said to leave him alone or they would have me to deal with too. Well, the three jumped on me and the kid I was trying to help ran home and left me. We rolled all over the ground fighting and I finally went home all scratched up and dirty. My Mom beat my butt but my Dad felt it wasn't right having three against one. He marched me off down to the boy's house, knocked on the door and when the boy's mother came to the door he told her what had happened and told her to send them out one at a time, but she refused. My Dad was proud of me that night. I think the boy's names were David and Jerome Finley, I can't remember the older brother's name. David grew up and became a minister. He married the girl across the street from me, Barbara Moss, who was a very good friend of mine; more about her later. I don't know what happened to Jerome or his older brother.

We did the usual things at Halloween knocking on doors and playing tricks on people. Back then we had some powerful fireworks too. One was called a cherry bomb and was a real blaster. We would take a pipe, shove one end in the ground at an angle, drop in a lighted cherry bomb then put a can over the end and watch it fly. One Halloween some kids, not me of course, put one in a neighbor's mailbox and closed the lid. Well, I want you to know it blew the entire mail box wide open. They don't sell cherry bombs like those anymore.

Me, my sister Evie, and Dad in Rock Hill, S.C.
around 1950.

Working & Making Money

Shortly after we had moved into our house, Dad bought the two lots on either side of us (one on Williams Street and one on Lewis Street). Within the first two years he built houses on each lot and sold them. Again, the push was to try and make money so the family could have a better life.

We all had been taught from a very early age to work hard. If you wanted something, you didn't expect someone to give it to you. You worked for it or you made it, like I did with my bicycle or a pole for pole vaulting. We made our own sling shots, bows and arrows, wooden pistols with a clothes pin and rubber band for shooting, and I even made a golf club once. A golf driving range up the road from us opened and sometimes in our ramblings we would pick up some of the stray balls. So I cut down a small tree with the roots on it, trimmed it and shaped the bottom like a golf club. I had seen the clubs people used and I copied that idea as best I could. It worked too and I could hit a ball with it, although not very good. The point is, if you wanted something you figured out how to get it.

Making money came pretty easy for me. I had a newspaper route delivering the local paper "The Evening Herald" and I also sold "The Grit" newspaper. Selling razor blades to all the workmen up at the bunk house as well as the ones who were staying at our house brought in some extra money too. I sold Cloverine salve, an ointment good for just about anything, and even ordered a course in taxidermy because I wanted to try my hand at stuffing a bird. I didn't have much luck at that though.

When the newspapers were delivered to Williams Grocery store next to the bunk house on Highway 21 I would go there, roll them up, and put rubber bands around them. I got to know Mr. Williams pretty good too. One day he was in the back doing something when I walked in the store so I went to the checkout area, got a pack of lifesavers and put them in my pocket. A little later when he came back I reached in my pocket to show him the dime bank I had bought to keep all my dimes in. Well Sir, guess what I pulled out. . . the lifesavers! I was a fast thinker though and said, "Oh I got these" and paid him for them. He knew I stole them, but he never said a word. I learned a valuable lesson.

Around 1950, right after World War II, a building boom started because all the men were coming back, getting married, and needed a place to live. As a result, a big housing development was started known as Rock Hill Homes. Dad began working on these houses putting siding on and I remember helping. Asbestos shingles were still the new thing. We worked on hundreds of these houses and all of them were covered with asbestos shingles. There are many homes even today that have these shingles. Of course asbestos is no longer used in any form because it has been linked to cancer.

As I got a little older, like fourteen, I started working at a drive-in restaurant called The Dutch Mill. It was built just like an old Dutch windmill with the wind propellers and everything, they didn't turn of course. I worked outside, 'hopping curb' it was called, where I would go to the cars, take orders and turn them in at the window. The window was exactly that, a regular window with a box made on the outside. The workers on the inside would push the window up and take and fill your order. When it was ready they would ring a bell and we would check at the window to make sure it was ours. We usually knew about when it would be ready though. We would then carry it to the car on a metal tray that hooked on the window. The arm underneath would swing up against the door and hold the tray steady. The ticket and money had to be taken back to the window and turned in. We got to keep our tips though. We sold lots of beer and even though I was fourteen nobody said anything about it. The rules were pretty lax back then.

After working outside for a while the owners, two brothers we called Mr. Harry and Mr. Clyde (I never did know their last name), asked me to come and work inside helping them. I mainly worked the window, passing out food, putting the drinks on the tray, and collecting money. To get the beer and soft drinks you had to reach down into a long drink box that had been filled with beer and drinks and covered with ice. As the ice melted, the box became half full of ice water. After reaching down in the water and fishing around to find the drink or beer you were looking for, your arm was freezing. This wasn't so bad in the summer time though because this place had no air conditioning.

I had one other duty and that was to go upstairs and change the movie film in the 16 mm projector. You see, we had a movie screen mounted out back on two telephone poles and showed all kinds of movies once it got dark. There was a hole cut through the roof with a top over it to keep the rain out for the movie to be projected through. We showed mostly cartoons and travel type films. Mr. Harry and Mr. Clyde were very nice to work for. I think I must have worked there several summers. I even bought a 22 pump rifle from Mr. Clyde. It was about the size of an air rifle. I don't remember how much it was but it sure was a pretty thing. After I was married and times were very tight, I pawned it in Charlotte, North Carolina for $10.00 and never got it back. I hate that.

The Dutch Mill 1950

The Dutch Mill was in the middle of this parking lot and in front of the arched sign. That is the same sign board we used to show the movies on. It did not have the crown then and it was painted white.

My High School Years

When I started high school I was smaller than most of the other kids. I did not do well in school. I was picked on and my fighting spirit had changed, I did not fight back. My teeth were very bad in that a lot of my teeth were missing. I still had my baby teeth in the front because my grown up teeth had never developed to push them out. Where my baby teeth had fallen out in other places, the grown up teeth never developed to fill the space. I remember some of the boys calling me snaggle tooth Sam. In glee club the boys behind me would thump my ears. My ears were kind of big back then, still are. As a result of these things, I became very self conscious and sort of withdrew. I did not have anything to do with girls either. I guess I was just shy and afraid to ask a girl for a date. I did not go to any of the school dances and stuff. I just felt left out.

Things got so bad in high school that my Mom had had enough. She took me to a dentist, and had my front baby teeth pulled and a partial plate put in. The Dentist said I had a condition in my jaw which he called "a mild occlusion" where the jaw bone is deformed so the bottom teeth do not touch the top teeth. Two of my three daughters inherited the same condition.

I did not get involved in sports at all. I guess I didn't feel included very much and since I was never asked, I didn't try. My teeth situation may have played a part, I don't know. I have never felt comfortable smiling. I can see now in my older years how these events have shaped my life.

My grades were poor and I had trouble following and understanding the lessons. I could not get help at home because Dad had only gone through the fourth grade and Mom through the sixth. I remember asking the teacher questions though. They would give a quick explanation and ask, "Now do you understand?" but I didn't so after a while I just gave up and sat in class with my mind on other things.

I remember sketching cartoon characters in a spiral notebook. Pluto, Mickey Mouse, Alley Oop, Bugs Bunny and others with each character filling a full page. I have no idea where that book went and with proper training I may have become an artist. Of course, I do get into drawing later in life, although of a different kind.

A number of times I skipped school. Once I went with two other boys in the woods and spent the day shooting walnuts out of trees with our 22 rifles. Another day I just walked across the street and laid down in the back seat of a friend's car until school was out. Sometimes I would leave school early, walk home about four miles away and time it so I would get home about the same time as the bus would have dropped me off. High school was not a great time for me.

English was one of my worst subjects. I have to give credit to my English teacher Mrs. Williamson though for taking time after class on numerous occasions to help me. I will always remember her showing me how to diagram a sentence. I also remember sitting in English class writing a poem about my old car, entitled "Nuts Over You." You will find it in the Lewis family poem book along with many other poems written by me, and some by my children. Some I think are very good.

What the heck, since it was my first poem I'm going to put it here. See what you think. The irony is I wrote this in my English class where I was having so much trouble with my grades. It rhymes with Twinkle, Twinkle, Little Star.

Nuts Over You

Rattle! Rattle! In my car,
How I wonder where you are.
In the door? The dash? The seat?
Near my head? My hands? My feet?
Are you inside, are you out?
Do you maybe move about?

Rattle! Rattle! In my car,
Are you near or are you far?
Are you metal? Are you glass?
Will you linger? Will you pass?
Are you bolts or springs I sigh,
Are you nuts, or else am I?

In the eleventh grade I took a metal shop class but did not like it. The one class I really liked and did well in was woodshop. I took woodshop in the twelfth grade, got a job at Glover's Cabinet Shop and received a grade on my work there. I was even allowed to leave school early and work about three hours in the afternoon. My teacher was Mr. O.S. Baldwin but we all called him "Zero."

Another time I remember working after school at Castle and Whiteside's Furniture store on Trade Street putting furniture together for display and driving their truck trying to collect payments from people. Very few people made their payments on time and most of them lived in the poorer parts of town.

I remember one time when I was out collecting payments I was driving through the black section of town in the hot summertime. I was thirsty so I stopped at a restaurant night club kind of place and went in and asked for a soft drink. This was a black establishment but I did not think a thing about it. The guy handed me a drink, I paid for it and left. I had no feelings one way or the other regarding blacks. The fact that blacks and whites went to different schools was just how it was. In fact, no blacks lived in the whole community of farms where I grew up so I had no interaction with blacks at all and in Rock Hill it was the same way. As a matter of fact it stayed that way until the schools were integrated. Anyway, after getting something to drink I got back in the truck and went about doing my job of collecting more payments. This job did not last long though and back to Glover's Cabinet Shop I went.

Rock Hill High School 1963

Often at lunch time some of the kids from school would walk uptown and get something to eat from different places. One of my favorites was Watkins News Stand on Trade Street. It was about eight feet wide at the street and maybe forty feet deep. It got narrower the further you went toward the back. The magazines were in thin racks on each wall all the way to the ceiling and they had a stick with a clip to get them down. This place also sold hotdogs, the best hotdogs in town. What made them so good was his special chili. Many times I would get a chili dog.

Next door was a pawn shop and I would always look in the window at things for sale. There was a big hunting knife that I just loved, so I saved my money and bought it for about ten dollars. I still have that knife although it's not as pretty now because I broke the bone handle trying to learn how to throw it. I still have the original leather sheath but it's in pretty bad shape. Maybe I will put a new bone handle on it and make a new leather sheath for it one day. What makes this knife so special is it was made in Solingen, Germany right after World War II around 1950. It is made of Solingen steel, the best steel in the world at that time. It will hold an edge better than any knife I have ever had. I even cut the top out of a steel barrel with it one time and it did not gap the blade.

Hannah's Hot Dogs on Trade Street
Rock Hill, SC 1971

The small awning in the middle is Watkins News Stand. It was wedged between two buildings. The pawn shop where I bought the knife (mentioned above) is on the right.

In the eleventh grade I was taking ninth, tenth, and eleventh grade classes. In the twelfth grade I thought I would graduate with the others and had planned for my cap and gown, then found out I did not have enough credits to graduate. When I found this out, I just quit and did not finish out the term. I eventually did graduate, but I will talk about that in a little bit. Later that year I left for Atlanta, Georgia to study radio and TV repair, which I knew a little something about. I will tell you about that later too.

Me leaving school

My senior picture

Left to right: Me, Mendel, and Furman. The little fellow is
our nephew Stan Shultz, our sister's boy. This was just before
I went to Atlanta for Radio and TV school.

First Girlfriends!!

I was sort of slow on having girlfriends although I do remember a girl that lived on the next street over from Williams Street which was Cedar Grove Lane. Her name was Mary Alice Buffkin. I was about fifteen years old at the time and carved her name in a big tree over behind her house. She never saw it though. I liked her and she must have liked me because I remember her giving her brother some money to ride on ahead with his bike so we could be alone. At the time I didn't have a clue.

I cannot think of another girl I had an attachment too before going to Atlanta when I was eighteen. Of course there was Barbara Moss that lived across the street. I spent some time with her but we were just friends more than anything else. Barbara wrote a nice note in my high school annual that I did not pay any attention to until I began to write this narrative. I was going through photo albums and my high school annuals looking for pictures for this book when I noticed the note she had written. After reading it, I realized that she cared for me a lot more than I did her. It is on the next page, read it and see what you think. She ended up marrying David Finley, one of the boys I got in a fight with at the drive-in movie theater I told you about. He lived down the street and later became a preacher. I did see a girl or two when I was in Atlanta but more about that later.

As you know by now, I was always interested in how things worked and since I was always messing with Mom's radio it just made sense that I would be good at working on radios and things. In the spring of 1954, a girl stopped by the house who worked for a radio and TV repair school in Atlanta, Georgia. She and others were traveling around the south getting people signed up to start school that summer. She did a real selling job to my Dad and the fact that she was very good looking probably helped as far as my Dad was concerned. She started out asking if anyone in the family had an interest in radios and TVs. Of course they said I was and then she put the sales pitch on; she was very good. It would cost $600 for me to go and that included my room and board at a big house run by a retired Sea Captain in Atlanta. The school was scheduled to start in June of 1954. Of course I wanted to go and Mom and Dad agreed and signed the papers.

Near the end of my high school year when I saw I didn't have enough credits to graduate, I quit and before you knew it I was on a bus for Atlanta and though I had never traveled anywhere before, it did not bother me.

****

The note from Barbara

Dear Sam, I don't know how to start this because as I write this I realize that you aren't the same thirteen year old boy I used to know, but almost grown. Strange how the years flew. It doesn't seem possible that you won't be going to school or I won't see you this summer. I've always brought my problems and worries to you.

I sincerely hope you'll have the best of everything in the future because you deserve everything you'll ever get.

When you're gone, I don't know who I'll bring my problems to. Even though you don't think I'll miss you, I will. I'll miss you more than you think. The best of everything to you.

Always "is" forever
Love Barbara

P.S.
You'd better write me this summer while you're in Atlanta and I'll write you. I'm not kidding.

May the Good Lord bless and keep you til we meet again.
****

There now is that not sweet or what.

Life in Atlanta

I arrived in Atlanta and got off the bus at 1300 Ponce De Leon Avenue, my new home while I would be going to school. I was excited and looking forward to this new adventure.

The picture below was taken from Google Earth.

1300 Ponce De Leon Avenue
The house has been torn down and this complex put in its place.

I walked up to the house, knocked on the door and was told to come in. I introduced myself to an older man whom I found out later had been a ship's Captain in the Navy. I was shown around the place, where I would be sleeping, and told all about meals. There were a lot of guys staying here that were going to the radio and TV school.

The next day we showed up at the school. We walked of course, even though it was probably two miles. While I was in Atlanta I walked a lot or hitch-hiked. The school was in a large building on the second floor above several retail stores located on Peachtree Street. Classes were being held in the evenings and I was told if you wanted to get a job you could. Everything was explained to me about the classes which were to start the next day. Afterward, I decided I might as well look for a job so I walked down the street to check everything out. About a block away was the Loew's Grand Theatre and next door to the theatre was the Orange Teaco, an ice cream and soda shop that also sold taffy candy. You could watch the taffy being made because there was a show window up front with a little machine that had two prongs going around and around each other. Now picture this glob of taffy on the prongs and it is being stretched over and over as the two prongs go around each other. Pretty eye catching and tempting.

The Orange Teaco is where ten cents would get you a "one of a kind Orange Teaco drink," and fifteen cents would get you a fabulous chocolate malt. Blending two cups of orange juice with two teaspoons of sugar and four tablespoons of powdered coffee creamer will closely resemble the Orange Teaco drink. Remember to add a dash of nutmeg on top too.

I thought working at the Orange Teaco would be fun so I applied for a job the next day and was hired, I guess my past experience working at the Dutch Mill in Rock Hill when I was a teenager helped. So I went to work there the following day. My work consisted of putting the fresh teaco mixture into the refrigerated dispenser so it could start getting cold and ready to serve before we opened for business. The owner made the mixture so he could keep the exact ingredients secret. We also sold malts and milk shakes. Unlike the ingredients I mentioned above, the real Orange Teaco drink was made from fresh orange juice and some other secret ingredients thought to be sugar and powdered coconut, mixed together and frozen into slush in a machine that had a spiral inside a tube. Outside, the tube was refrigerated and as the juice froze the spiral would scrap it off until the entire mixture was semi-frozen. It came out of the front of the tube by a valve. When opened, a glass was filled and it was served with a straw. Man was it good. All of that orange flavor with a hint of coconut was a favorite for many people and we sold lots of it. At the end of the day everything had to be cleaned which meant taking the dispenser apart and cleaning it real good.

By the way, there was no bathroom at the Orange Teaco, so with permission we used the Loew's Grand Theatre's restrooms next door. I got to know the ticket takers that way.

I would work at the Orange Teaco during the day and go to school at night. One day someone paid with a silver dollar, but on closer inspection I noticed it had a face on it that looked Chinese so I put a dollar in the cash register and kept it. I carried it in my pocket for many years until the face on it was about worn off. It must be pure silver. I still have it with some other coins I have saved over the years.

The following photos are of the area near where I worked and a little history of the places.

DeGive's - 1893

As it looked in 1939

Margaret Mitchell arriving at the World Premiere Gala of "Gone with the Wind" - 1939

Before it was the Loew's Grand Theatre, the building on Peachtree Street was Laurent DeGive's Grand Opera House. Built in 1893, as shown above, it was remodeled in 1923 to become the Loew's Grand Theatre. It was here that the Gala World Premiere of "Gone with the Wind," written by Margaret Mitchell of Atlanta, was held in 1939. The premiere of "Gone with the Wind" at the Loew's Grand

Theatre on December 15, 1939 brought Hollywood to Atlanta.

The Loew's Grand Theatre was listed on the National Register of Historic Places in 1977 and was last used for storage. It was damaged by a fire in January 1978 and later torn down. The theater was memorialized by Davis Cone's painting which can be viewed in *Popcorn Palaces: The Art Deco Movie Theater Paintings of Davis Cone* (Kinerk & Wilhelm, 2001), and available from Harry N. Abrams books.

The first thing we got at school was a jacket with the name of the school on the back. The first thing we learned at school was the various parts of a radio and the color code. You see back then we didn't have circuit boards and chips that are being used today. All of the various parts were color coded so you could know what value each one had. Many looked very much alike so by knowing what each color stood for you would know what you needed to replace it with.

The radio we were learning about was a super heterodyne radio. To remember the color code we had to memorize a rhyme and while it is rather objectionable now, back then it's what they taught us. It went like this "Bad boys rape our young girls but violet gives willingly." The first letter of each word represented a color. It went, black, brown, red, orange, yellow, green, blue, violet, gray, white. At the end of our schooling we were told we would have to take a box of parts and assemble a radio. It would have to be done on a flat piece of plywood with each part mounted on the front and labeled with all wiring behind the board.

My work and classes continued, I continued to live on Ponce De Leon Avenue, and I was learning a lot. After a few months, I decided to go home to Rock Hill so I walked out to the street one afternoon and started hitchhiking. Catching a ride back then right after the war was not a problem because most people would pick you up. Late in the afternoon, I was into my third ride with some people who were going to a town that was on my way. By the time we got to this town it was getting dark so I went into town with them and they let me off downtown. Well, this little town closed up at dark so I sat on a bench in front of a store until daybreak. I didn't even see a cop all night. I finally made it to Rock Hill that morning. Of course I hitchhiked all the way back to Atlanta on Sunday.

My Life at Lockheed Aircraft

Several of us at the radio and TV school had heard that Lockheed was looking for people so some of us applied and were hired. Lockheed Aircraft was located about twenty miles west of Atlanta, Georgia near the small town of Marietta. They offered me a job on second shift but I was going to school at night so that was a problem. I went to the school folks and they said they would be starting day classes soon so I could attend those classes which meant I could work the second shift job at Lockheed. In October of 1954 I went to work for Lockheed on the second shift, but the day classes never happened. In fact, my job at Lockheed was so good, I pretty much forgot about school. I held several different positions at Lockheed over a period of time so I'll describe each one as I go along.

My first job was in the fabrication department. In that department I worked with a woman who had started for Lockheed during the war and continued on when the war was over. Lots of women had to go to work during the war to help with the war effort because most of the young men were off somewhere fighting.

In the fabrication department we were building the C 130 Hercules, a transport plane for the Army. Our job was to put the metal skin on the outside. She would put the metal panel in place, drill a hole for the rivet, and put in a cletoe which was a spring loaded clip that went in the hole to hold the panel in place. After securing the panel in several places, she would drill all the rivet holes. There were a lot of rivet holes and they were spaced about one inch apart.

After that was completed she would insert a rivet and my job was to buck the rivet. You do this with a bucking bar, a piece of heavy metal with many angles and sides for getting into tight places. I would place the bar against the rivet and she would use a rivet gun against the rivet with me holding the bucking bar so the rivet would flatten out on my side. She would stop then I would look at the rivet to see if it was spread out enough for a tight fit. If it was correct, I would tap two times. If not, I would tap once and she would hit it some more. She knew about what was needed because she seldom had to hit it any more. The reason for the tapping was I was inside and she was outside and sometimes we could not see each other. One interesting thing I noticed at Lockheed was the floor, it was concrete but it had wooden 4x4's cut a couple of inches long and attached to the floor standing on end. It was done this way to make it quiet and to soften the blow if something was dropped.

By the way, when I first started at Lockheed I was living at the place on Ponce De Leon Avenue. It wasn't too long after that though that I moved in with four other fellows who were working for Lockheed. We rented a house in Atlanta and since one of them had a car, we would all ride to work together. There were two girls that a friend and I had been seeing who asked us to move in with them. The girl I was seeing was a basketball player and so tall I had to stand one step up to kiss her goodnight. Anyway, we decided we would be better off not doing that, a very wise choice.

One month later, I caught a bus home to Rock Hill for the weekend. When my visit to Rock Hill was over and I got back to Atlanta, all of our belongings were out on the pavement. Apparently the guy who was supposed to make the rent payment had not and the owner had my 22 rifle that I got when I was working at the Dutch Mill many years earlier. I had brought it with me when I went to Atlanta. I finally convinced him to let me have it and we went our separate ways.

Instead of staying on to live in Atlanta, which was twenty miles away from work, I decided to go to Marietta which is where Lockheed was actually located. I then moved into a little cheap motel sharing a room with another fellow I knew. After two weeks I found out he was writing bad checks using my radio and TV jacket as a prop so I moved on.

Before leaving the motel, a friend told me about a lady who had a 1939 Ford coupe for sale. It was her husband's car but he was locked up for hauling whiskey. She needed money and selling the car was a quick way to get it. You see, all this time I had been depending on others to get to work and back. With a car I could drive myself to and from work and also drive home to Rock Hill from time to time. It was a smart decision so I bought the car. I don't remember what I paid for the car but it wasn't much. So I moved out of the cheap motel and away from the guy who was writing bad checks and started looking for another place to stay.

I saw an ad in the paper for a room in a private home so I checked on it and moved in. That year, I remember going with the family's daughter to look for a Christmas tree out in the country in my car. She was about my age which was nineteen. Her parents must have thought well of me to ask me to take her. I think they kind of wanted to get us together but I was not interested. After the first of the year, I moved again but this time I moved in with a fellow from work that had moved his family, a wife and little girl, to Marietta. I had my own room but I slept on a pallet on the floor. I should have bought a cot but I never thought of it.

Before leaving the motel I bought a 1939 Ford coupe, like the one above. It had two round fold-up seats in the back.

Having my own car had its benefits but it also had its down side. Every time I went home the cops would stop me and the first thing they would say was "Open the trunk boy!!" but the only thing in the trunk was a bunch of old tires because I was always having flats. I ran slick tires most of the time because I could get them real cheap or for free. Anyway, the cops thought I was hauling whiskey and while I didn't know it at the time, the car was set up for hauling whiskey and the cops could spot it right away. I was stopped a lot for that reason.

Another time going home to Rock Hill, I was in the area of Chester, South Carolina when it starting raining. With the rain, I was concerned because of those slick tires. Then I came up on an older fellow driving real slow so I eased out and went around him. Well, when I turned back to the right lane I began to slide and spin. I did a slow 360 degree revolution down the middle of the road and when I was straight again I gave it a little gas and drove on down the road. I looked back and the man had pulled off of the road and stopped. It must have really scared him. I just kept on going.

Even with slick tires and being stopped by the cops, I really enjoyed that car. I remember one weekend a good friend of mine who worked with me at Lockheed wanted to go home, so I took him. He lived about halfway to Rock Hill in some little town, I can't remember where. I was staying at his house when a girl from next door came over and we started talking. The county fair was in town and she asked me to take her so we took off in my car. We had a very good time at the fair. She even tried her hand at one of the games and won a great big teddy bear. I have often wondered if the operator didn't let her have the big teddy bear because she was so pretty. On the way back she said "Let's stop so I can give you some sugar." Those were her words. I did, she did and we went on home. She was a little older than I was and knew her way around better than I did. Anyway, the next day my friend and I headed back to Marietta and I never saw that girl again.

Okay, now back to talking about the different jobs I had at Lockheed.

After working in the fabrication department, my next job at Lockheed was in the blueprint department with another person but in order to work there you had to be able to roller skate. Every part of the airplane had a drawing for it and if you were going to be working on a particular thing you had to get a print to go by. There must have been thousands of blueprints and each one was numbered and located in little bins. When a request came in for a particular print, we had to skate down these long aisles, find the correct print, and bring it up front where it was signed out. When the work was completed, the print had to be returned so we signed it back in and put it back in the bin it came from.

Then I moved on to the spot welding department where the metal parts had to be cleaned by dipping them in a vat of cleaning solution. We had to wear cotton gloves handling the metal. We used magnesium for some of the parts. If there was a smudge on the metal and you spot welded it, a hole would burn through where the smudge was. To clean a piece you would attach a cable with a clip in two different places then with a hand held control lift the piece up and lower it into the vat. After so many minutes you took it out and moved it to another vat to rinse it off. After drying, they were ready for spot welding. My job was doing the cleaning but sometimes I would do some spot welding.

Next, I was sent to the flight lines where I worked with a fuel crew. After each plane was built, or an existing plane was modified, it was sent to our area to be prepped before it went out for a test flight. Our job was to connect all the fuel lines and pumps as well as install the fuel liners or bladders. Everywhere fuel was stored in an airplane a rubber type bladder made to fit the space had to be installed.

To do this, we took the deflated bladder, shoved it into the space, ran a nylon cord through attachments on the outside of the bladder and through attachments located around the space. Then we crawled out and pulled the cord to stretch out the bladder so we could attach the fuel line. This was a very tedious job because fuel is stored in a lot of places on an airplane. Once all connections were complete we would put some fuel in and turn on a pump to check for leaks on different lines. When the fuel lines, pumps and liners were all in place and tested, a pilot would start the plane and take it up to check out all the systems.

One time another fellow and I were completing a fuel line hookup and someone in the cockpit flipped the wrong switch turning on a pump on the line we were working on. Fuel came gushing out all over us! We were in luck though because the pump was turned off real quick. Nevertheless, the situation created quite a commotion because we could have had a fire real easy. Lucky for us, all that happened was my buddy and I had to head for the showers to clean up and change into clean coveralls.

In the winter of 1954, I was sent over to do modifications to the B-47 Jet Bomber. They were so big they were parked on the tarmac with the front end inside what they called a nose hanger. The nose of the plane stuck into a tall building with canvas hanging like curtains draped around the body in front of the wings. The reason for this was to weather proof the cockpit since it was open. We had portable heaters with flexible ducts so we could have heat wherever we were working on the plane. We also had to install the fuel tank liners and bladders just like we did on the flight lines. These planes were being outfitted to carry the atomic bomb so special shackles were being installed to hold the bombs. These shackles could be released by a switch at the bombardier's location.

I also did work in the cockpit. On the backside of a panel I had to install a small pulley so a cable would run around and up to a handle that controlled something or other. This would not have been so hard except you had to reach behind a panel to do it and look in a mirror to see what you were doing. There was one place on the plane where another fuel bladder went in where they specifically picked me to do the job because I was real slim. The space was above the bomb bay and known as the "hell hole" because there was barely enough room to slide in on your stomach.

In March of 1955, while I was still working at Lockheed, some of my friends and I were approached by the Civil Service and asked if we would be interested in a job.

They were looking for a group of young single men to travel wherever they were needed in the world and to do modifications to certain planes. My draft status was a problem so they asked me to go to my draft board and see if I could get it changed, then they would take me on as part of the group. I went back home to Rock Hill that weekend and checked with my draft board, but was unable to get a change. When I reported back to the Civil Service people they said they could not hire me. So, all my friends left and afterwards I was by myself.

A few weeks passed and I decided to take another route in my life and got ready to head back home to Rock Hill. I got in touch with a fellow I knew from my time on the flight lines who had expressed an interest in buying my 1939 Ford coupe to haul whiskey. I sold it to him but why I sold it, I don't remember unless I needed the money. He didn't have the car long though. Several weeks later as he was leaving work, he was broadsided and tore the car up. Having sold my car, I left my job at Lockheed that spring and caught the bus back to Rock Hill.

Life Back in Rock Hill

When I got back to Rock Hill, I began looking for a job in a radio repair shop and also checked with Glover's Cabinet Shop cabinet shop where I had worked while in school. It turned out I could make more money at Glover's doing cabinet work so I got a job there.

Shortly after starting work at Glover's I bought another car, a 1940 Ford. The car had a gear shift on the floor, which was pretty standard back then and didn't cost extra, but I still needed $100 in order to buy the car. I remember asking my Dad to loan me the money and told him I would pay him back from money I was making working at Glover's. He said no and that if I wanted the car I should save up the money myself. I wanted this car bad though so I asked my older brother Lester to loan me the money. He was married and living in a house trailer behind Dad's house plus he had a job. I asked him for the money and he loaned it to me. Anyway, I got the car and spent most of my spare time working on it. There was always something breaking.

One night I got a phone call from two friends of mine. Robert Cotton and another fellow, whose name I can't remember, had been out in the country on a gravel road, went around a curve too fast in their car, slid in the ditch and flipped over. I went to their rescue and used my car to take them home so they could get someone to go out and turn it back over. I was pretty careful with my car, although I do remember one time I was out cruising as we did back then and pulled into Bob's Drive In, a hamburger place. There was a pile of gravel over next to the edge of the parking lot and when I was ready to leave I put it in reverse and backed up to turn around. Unfortunately, I did not see the gravel pile until it was too late. I rammed the rear bumper into the gravel and felt pretty stupid. It didn't hurt anything though, just my pride.

My 1940 Ford was the same as the model shown above

One day during the summer of 1955, I was out riding around in my car and happened to be going through a subdivision called Rock Hill Homes (I had worked there with my Dad) when I saw two girls. One I knew, her name was Raylene Smith, but I didn't know the other girl and paid no attention to her. I stopped to offer the two girls a ride and Raylene got in the front seat while the other girl rode in the back. I drove them to where they were going and went on about my way. That other girl, who was fifteen at the time, was the same girl I would later fall madly in love with and who would turn out to be my future wife Kay. I don't remember seeing Kay again until I met her at Glover's Cabinet Shop in May of 1956.

Kay at age 14

Kay around 1955/1956 at age 16 – six months before I met her at Glover's Cabinet Shop.

After working at Glover's for a while I began to think about my future. I think my experiences in Atlanta caused me to realize that I needed to finish high school. So in the fall of 1955, I went to see the principal at Rock Hill High School. His name was Mr. J.J. Godbold (we always referred to him as "The Man") and asked him if I could return and finish high school.

He was hesitant to let me come back to school since I was 20 years old but I explained to him about my time in Atlanta and that I really wanted to finish high school. He finally let me start back, even though I would be starting six weeks late into the second semester. He agreed to let me take the classes with the understanding that I would study hard, make up the six week's worth of work and keep my grades up. I thanked him, made up the missed time and completed the year with good grades and plans to go to summer school so I could get my diploma. During the fall of 1955 and the spring of 1956 my life was school, working, and dating. I had finally become truly interested in girls.

Mr. J.J. Godbold aka "The Man"

While at Glover's Cabinet Shop in Rock Hill, I remember building shelving units for a library that was in another town in South Carolina. When we had the shelving units completed, Mr. Glover, Jerry Turner (a really good friend of mine), and myself went to the other town to do the installation. We all stayed at a rooming house that night where we had a real family style meal, good country cooking. Jerry and I had a lot of fun times together.

While we were installing the shelving units at the library, Jerry ended up meeting some girl and wanted to see her that night. He asked me to go with him so we took the cabinet shop's truck and drove out to her house. Since Jerry was the one who had asked to see her, I stayed in the truck the whole time he was inside. That was a long wait. There was another time when Jerry and I were out together and went by a girl's house. Well, Jerry went in but I stayed in the car just like before. Except this time I had a small bottle of wine that I kept sipping on. After a while though, I got very sick and threw up. Later, when Jerry came back out, all I wanted to do was go home.

I saw quite a few girls during this period and one of them was Rosemary Parrish. Later when Kay found out I had dated Rosemary she didn't like it. Maybe she knew something I didn't know. Another time, Jerry and I had asked two girls from Charlotte to go to a dance with us. The dance was near where they lived on the south side of Charlotte and near the trailer park where my girl lived. We went to the dance but didn't dance much and when we got ready to leave, my girl was already gone. She left with someone else I guess. In fact, I have no idea where she went or how she even got home.

One thing popular with a lot of young people back then was going to the dam at the river. Well, one time Jerry and I went out to the dam with two girls. I remember how we all walked down by the river and my girl started walking away into some willow trees where she and I could be by ourselves. Poor me, I made no moves on her. I sure missed a lot of chances.

There was one other girl I saw, I say "saw" because I never was allowed to actually take her anywhere. Her father and mother were Jehovah Witnesses and the only way I could see her was at her house, which meant there was always someone in the room with us. Needless to say that didn't last too long.

One more girl that I dated a few times had long hair and was very pretty. She was a Preacher's daughter and you know what they say about Preacher's daughters. Well, it was not true with me but I found out later from several others, it was true.

Meeting My Future Wife - Kay

One Saturday in late May of 1956, my friend Jerry Turner and I were in Glover's Cabinet Shop working on a boat we were building. This boat was a specially designed boat with molding down the side that matched the trim on a 1955 Ford. The boat was not large but it had lots of speed features. We ended up painting the boat sky blue and the natural oak trim on the side really set it off. It was only twelve feet long but with the ten-horsepower Mercury motor it would fly and could actually pull someone on water skis. The boat was very stable too. I remember Jerry trying to turn it over by running it wide open and turning it as hard as he could but all it would do was skip across the water. What a boat.

Anyway, while we were working on the boat, the loading dock door was open and we saw two young girls walking along the road. We called them over and started talking and found out that they were later going to go for a ride with a sister that could drive. We told them to stop by and we would go for a ride with them so a little later they showed up. The sister, Kay, who was driving, and the other two girls got out and came over to the loading dock. Kay had dark brown hair and the biggest blue eyes I had ever seen. I was smitten and could not take my eyes off her. I asked Kay if she would like to see the boat we were building. She said yes and since the loading dock was a little high, I reached down to take her hand to help her up into the shop. Once she was in I continued to hold her hand until she pulled away.

We talked for a while and the girls said they were going up to a hamburger place to get something to drink. We asked if we could go with them and they said okay so Jerry and I went to wash up because we were dusty and had been sweating. While we were washing up, I told Jerry I was going to marry her. It was love at first sight. Well maybe second sight, since I had met her once before.

When we got to the car I got in the front with Kay. However, much later after we were married Kay told me she had really wanted Jerry to get up front because my holding her hand had bothered her. An interesting side note, when we got to the car, Kay was driving, but her sister Debra and their friend Peggy Wallace were in the back seat. I guess the open front seat was an invitation meant for Jerry but I got there first and took the front seat. We all went to get something to drink and later the girls dropped us off back at the shop. After this, I thought about Kay all the time. Every time I would see her at school, I would ask her for a date, but she always had an excuse. We finished out that school year and started summer school but I didn't give up and kept asking.

Then sometime in July 1956 on a Saturday evening I was out with Barbara Moss. Remember her? She was my friend from across the street that wrote me that nice note. Anyway, we had been cruising and got back home about 7:20 pm. When I went inside, my Mother said a Kay Riley had called and said something about a date we were suppose to have had at 7:00 pm. Well, I didn't remember a date but figured with what I was hearing she obviously must have said yes one time out of all the times I had asked. I was always asking her and I was so used to hearing her say "no" I must have missed it. Well, it didn't matter I was just so pleased it had finally happened.

I took a quick shower, changed clothes, jumped in my car and took off to Kay's house. After I picked her up, we went to one of the drive-in burger places and sat and talked. We had a very nice evening and after that we dated regularly. One Saturday night we went out to the lake to "watch the submarine races." Of course there were no races, we just sat, looked at the lake and talked. Finally, my charm was working and she was becoming smitten too. We went to church a lot too because her parents didn't have a problem with her going out during the week, as long as it was going to church.

On the weekends we would go to the movies or over to my Mom's, or even visit my sister Alma and her husband John. Sometimes we would just go out to get a burger at one of the drive-ins. There were plenty of drive-ins back then and one of the favorites was called the "Bob-In." Another spot was "The Park-In" and of course there was the place out near the Catawba River on highway 21 called "Johnny Porter's." It was off limits to all the young people, especially the Winthrop College girls. "Johnny Porter's" had curb service and privacy stalls where you could park. Needless to say I never took Kay there.

The Park-In

The Bob-In

Johnny Porter's

Kay and I dated on through the summer as we went to summer school, and I finally received my high school diploma. An interesting thing about my diploma is that I was told to take it to Mr. Godbold so he could sign it. He was sick though and I never did have him sign it. So does that mean I didn't finish high school? Anyway, during that summer and fall Kay and I continued to see each other and before we knew it we began talking about getting married. At the time Kay was only sixteen.

We continued to date through Christmas and as a Christmas present I gave her a walnut heart-shaped jewelry box with an engagement ring in it. By January of 1957, when Kay turned seventeen, we began to seriously plan on getting married so I decided to ask her Mom and Dad for their approval. Her Dad said okay but as I remember it, her Mom said "Over my dead body." Kay remembers it a bit differently but the bottom line answer was "No!" So, we decided to run off and get married and began planning our wedding.

We needed to get a marriage license though. So, on a date night, we drove down to a Justice of the Peace who lived in Chester, South Carolina. Her name was Hattie Harden. We had already found out she would give marriage licenses without asking too many questions.

Running Off & Getting Married

We planned for the wedding to be on a Friday night, March 15, in a church we had visited several times. It was there at Four Square Gospel Church that my family and a few friends witnessed the proceedings. After the ceremony, Kay and I left for Charleston, South Carolina for our honeymoon. Kay had already taken clothes from her house so we were all set to leave right after the wedding. I had my Sister Evie call Kay's Mom after we had left though. Evie was the one who let her know what we had done.

We drove down to Charleston, S.C. and had a nice weekend, going to the museum and other sites around the area. On our way back, we saw a cousin of mine and stopped on the road and had a visit. After getting back to Rock Hill, we went to Kay's Mother's house and picked up the rest of Kay's clothes. I don't think her Mom had anything to say to her so we went to my Mom's house and stayed there for about two weeks.

At the end of two weeks, we found and rented a small apartment on Confederate Avenue just for the two of us. Our early marriage began at this place. It was upstairs and it was small. The area we used as a bedroom was so small we had trouble getting a bed into it. I don't remember where we got the furniture from. We had a small living/dining area and a kitchen area hardly big enough to turn around in. But it was home, we were together, and we were happy.

Our wedding picture in Rock Hill, S.C.
March 15, 1957

Upstairs apartment on Confederate Avenue.
The first place we called home.

When Kay and I got married, I was working at Glover's Cabinet Shop making one dollar an hour. The problem was, business at the cabinet shop had gotten real slow. Mr. Glover even began making simple wooden boats and stacking them out front for sale. However, by early summer he said he didn't have anything else for me to do.

One Saturday I began looking for another job and ended up in Charlotte, North Carolina checking with any place I saw in my travels. By late afternoon, I stopped at a hosiery mill on Worthington Avenue on the south side of Charlotte and then continued walking down the street. There in front of me was Carolina bakery so I went in and asked for a job. I was getting desperate and would take a job doing just about anything. Of course they had nothing for me so I just walked out front, saw a building across the street with the front door open, and headed over there. I had decided this was going to be my last stop for the day as it was getting late and I was ready to head home. I didn't even look up to see the name of the business, I just went in.

There was an office on the left so I stopped and knocked on the door. Even though this was a Saturday the Secretary and the Manager were both there so I asked to speak to the Manager. When he came out I introduced myself, told him I was looking for a job, and that I would do any kind of work. He then said "Let's walk through the plant." At this point, I did not know what kind of place this was but as we stepped into the plant from the office I was shocked. There in front of me was a fixture plant (a commercial cabinet shop) with all of the same equipment I was already familiar with from building cabinets, the one thing I really knew how to do. This was Morgan Fixture Company.

The Manager and I walked through the shop and I began to tell him everything I knew something about. I also expressed to him my interest in drafting because he had already shown me the drafting room where the drawings were done for all of the things they built. He must have been impressed because he told me if I would come in and learn all of the various jobs, he would give me a chance to work in the drafting room. However, he did say I would need to talk to his Foreman because that was who did all the hiring. So, two days later on a Monday in June of 1957, I went back, talked with the Foreman, and he put me to work.

God was preparing me for the future.

Shortly after going to work for Morgan Fixture Company, Kay and I moved to a small apartment on Williams Street and near my Mom's house.

On the right is our apartment on Williams Street.

During this time, Russia sent the space satellite Sputnik into orbit. It was October of 1957 and I remember calling my Dad to tell him about the satellite. When I was a kid, he had always told people, "Sam's going to the moon." After hearing about Sputnik, I figured the moon would not be far off and was something I always thought about. In fact, Kay's Mother gave me a clear plastic sphere for Christmas one year that has always been special to me. The sphere sits on top of a base, and inside the sphere are stars, the moon and a tiny plastic rocket ship. The caption reads, "For our trip to the moon." I still have that sphere.

When man finally landed on the moon in July of 1969, I was up late that night in front of the TV with my windup movie camera filming it as it happened. That film has been preserved and is now part of our family home movies. Of course, landing on the moon was a big news story and the Charlotte newspaper published a book with pictures and a story about the event and called it, *Footprints on the Moon*. I bought two copies of the book and inside the front cover of one I wrote a long note to my Dad about how I had always thought this would happen. Then I gave it to him. After he and my Mother had died I asked about the whereabouts of the book. Unfortunately, I have never learned where it ended up.

My first job at Morgan was to go down under the floor where the coal fired furnace was. I would crawl inside the furnace and clean it out in preparation for firing it up for the winter. From that dirty beginning I would end up working in every area of the plant. After my job working on the furnace, I worked in the lumber room sorting out the different size pieces so they could be cut, planed and sized. After that, I worked in the machine room where the lumber was sized and shaped. I was able to work on all of the machines including one where large flat pieces of wood were sanded. This was done on a special sander consisting of a very long six inch wide sand belt which ran around rollers at both ends and a rolling platform under the belt. The material was placed on the platform and moved back and forth as a block of wood was pressed down on the smooth side of the sand belt. The block could be moved up and down the belt to cover a large area.

From there I worked in the assembly area. By this stage of the construction process, everything was pretty much cut to size and only needed to be put together. However, all of the molding had to be sanded by hand. You guessed it; that was my job. You see, I was new and the old craftsman felt they had to train me so sanding was my first job. I would sand all day by hand until my fingers felt like they would bleed. There was no plastic laminate back then, everything was wood. There was no fancy glue either. We used hide glue from a small hot pot. It was made from animal hides and smelled just awful.

I also worked in the finishing room where everything was sprayed with hot lacquer and then hand rubbed with oil and ground up pumas stone for a very smooth and slick finish. It was in this area of the plant that I learned how to use the spray guns and how to get a nice smooth finish on the cabinets. We sprayed with hot lacquer, which meant the lacquer went through a heating element before it reached the spray gun. Having the lacquer hot made it smooth out better. On a vertical surface you always started at the bottom and worked your way up. This gave the layer you were spraying something to "sit" on. This may not make sense but you got a better finish by doing it this way.

When the lacquer was first sprayed onto the cabinet, it would dry with a slight textured finish. The goal of hand rubbing was to remove that rough texture. We either used a felt block or a piece of burlap folded to make a pad. The pad was dipped into oil and pumas and then the rubbing began. As you rubbed you would stop every so often and, with your thumb, wipe the oil away to see if you had rubbed enough to remove the rough texture. You had to be careful and not go all the way through the finish. This was very messy work. So bad in fact that we wore rubber aprons.

The whole time I worked at Morgan's I was very inquisitive and everyone would show me how to do things. During this time, Kay was working too. In fact, she was able to find a job in Rock Hill working at Taylor's Super Market as a cashier. Things were going along just fine.

Moving to Charlotte & Disappointment

With me working in Charlotte, Kay and I felt we should be closer to work so we moved to Charlotte into an apartment in Tryon Hills. I continued working at Morgan's Fixture Company and Kay began working at a dress shop called The Vogue. However, sometime in December of 1957, Kay got pregnant and lost her job at The Vogue. So, we started looking for another place where the rent was cheaper.

In January of 1958, we found a place out west of Charlotte on Thrift Road and moved in. This place was a converted convenience store and service station and was divided into three rooms, a living room, kitchen and a bedroom. We stayed there through the winter. It was really cold that year.

We did not have a stove so we cooked on a hot plate and ate beans a lot. During the winter we ran out of heating oil, our car broke down, and I was put on short time, about twenty hours a week. Kay did find a job working as a cashier at a discount store but we had practically no money. So here was Kay pregnant and going to work with no money. Things were so bad that for lunch she would "snitch" a pack of crackers (that sounds better than stealing) and usually one of the fellows working there would buy her a drink. At one point, Kay's Mom came up and bought us some oil so we could have some heat. She also had an electric stove delivered. Meanwhile, I'm still hanging on at Morgan's and continuing to dream about working in the drafting room.

We lived in the place on Thrift Road through the rest of the winter but finally, with help from Kay's Mom, by April of 1958, we moved back to Rock Hill and into a farm house on Eden Terrace. By this time I was back to having forty hours a week at Morgan Fixture Company, but I was still working in the cabinet room sanding or hand rubbing the fixtures in the finish room.

At Morgan when break time came, everybody would gather around where the drink machines were. This area was

113

just outside the drafting room and had glass windows overlooking the shop. I was forever looking in there and imagining myself sitting and drawing, and wearing nice slacks and a shirt instead of what I usually wore to work. The fellows from the drafting room would stand around with us on break so I began asking questions to one of the draftsmen telling him I wanted to learn how to draw. He would explain things to me and show me how they went about drawing different parts of the fixtures. One day he gave me something to draw, so I went home and began working on it.

I had already made a small drawing board and tee square because you needed those to do the type of drawing I wanted to learn. Kay had even given me a set of drawing instruments the year before because of my interest in drawing. I still have those drawing instruments by the way. Anyway, I worked on the drawing and would take it back to the draftsman, and he would show me what I needed to change. Slowly I learned.

In June of 1958, after about a year working there, I felt it was time for my shot at the drafting room. I went to the manager and showed him some of my drawings and asked him about going to work in the drafting room like he had promised. Well, I must have caught him at a bad time because he was very short with me and told me that I should just go back out in the shop and go back to work. This really upset me, so I went back to my work bench and told the guys I was quitting. I took a large rolling tool box I had built, packed my things, and rolled my box to the loading dock. Jim Moore and Henry Wright, two fellows I worked with that had become friends of mine came over and asked what was going on. They knew about the promise that had been made to me and how I had been practicing my drawing, so they helped me load my tool box and I left. From what I learned later I think the reason the Manager acted the way he did was the company was in financial trouble and that was on his mind, not me. That actually worked to my benefit later on.

Tryon Hills Apartments
Our first place in Charlotte, N.C.

Moving Back to Rock Hill

After quitting my job at Morgan Fixture Company, and now that we were back living in Rock Hill, I decided to go and see Mr. Williams at Williams' Cabinet Shop where I had worked part-time before. He took me on part-time so I began working for him as well as other jobs I could find. Winthrop College was having a science lab put in and the company doing the installation was in need of people to help get it done. That particular job only lasted about a month though. Afterward, when I went back to Williams' Cabinet Shop, I was given full-time work.

Our first child, Sammie Kay, was born in August of 1958 while we were living in the farm house on Eden Terrace. In the spring of 1959 we moved again, this time to be near Kay's Mom on Caruthers Avenue. We were able to get this house because the owners knew Kay's Mother. They wanted someone that would take care of the place while they were in another state working and Kay's Mom had suggested us. Meanwhile, I continued to work at Williams' Cabinet Shop and any thought of Morgan Fixture Company and the drafting room was forgotten

Later on, I applied for and got a job at the Celanese Plant where I could make a little more money. Money always drove me just so we could try and pay the bills. The Celanese Plant made different types of synthetic yarn. My job was just as a laborer but with the need for money, I took it. When the yarn was made it came out of a tiny hole as a hot liquid way up high and dropped down through a clear box, where it was cooled. As it solidified it became this tiny little flexible thread that we call yarn. It was picked up and wound on a spinning bobbin moving at the same speed as the yarn was coming down. Once the bobbins were full, they were taken off and put on a special transport. This was a two sided steel frame on wheels with pegs on each side, which is where the bobbins were stacked. This is where my job came in. I pulled the transport over to an overhead moving track with hooks on it.

I put the transport in place, the track dropped down for three or four feet and hooked the transport at the top and away it went to another station where it was taken off and moved on to wherever it was going.

Coming in on the track from the opposite direction were transports with bobbins that had some yarn still on them. It was my job to pull those transports off, catch up the ends of the broken yarn, bundle them up and feed them into a suction port that pulled it off and ground it up. It was then sent back to be processed again. The danger in this job was when the suction began it was so strong it could yank a bobbin completely off the transport. You didn't want to be in front when that happened

One significant problem in working at the Celanese Plant were the chemicals they used. For processing the yarn, they used acetone and I breathed so much of it that when I would wake up at home, the bedroom would smell just like acetone. This happened enough times that I decided maybe I should find something else to do.

The National Guard

In the meantime, with my draft status being what it was I thought it would be a good idea to join the guard. The extra money would be a big help and my good friend Jerry Turner joined about the same time. Being in the Guard meant meetings once a month and going for two weeks of training each summer.

While in the Guard, we went to different places. One was Fort McClellan in Alabama. As an infantry unit, the first week we were in the field. This meant sleeping in tents in the woods, taking cold showers from water they pumped from the creek, and eating food in the dark that had a lot of black pepper in it. At least I thought it was black pepper. I found out later the "black pepper" was actually gnats. I also remember crawling out of my shelter one morning, shaking out my blanket and finding a dead scorpion. Apparently he had crawled in during the night and I had rolled over and smashed him.

Our Company Commander was young and liked to be out front when things were going on. With my interest in radios they made me his radio operator which sounded like a great thing but actually sometimes it wasn't so great. Being his radio operator meant I had to be with him everywhere he went. For example, during an exercise that required us to go through a swamp about three feet deep I had to be right with him. This also meant I was right there with the alligators and cottonmouth snakes in the swamp.

There were other instances where the going wasn't the safest too. I remember one time we were lined up in a straight line going up to take a hill in a live fire exercise. That's right! Real bullets! Anyway, the Captain was to my left and the fellow on my right had a BAR (Browning automatic rifle). With a BAR, when you were firing it on automatic it tended to pull left, so you had to hold on tight. Well, when we started firing, the fellow with the BAR cut loose and that rifle came right around to the left and directly over mine and the Captain's head. I hit the ground and stayed there until the Captain secured the weapon and took this fellow out of the line. That was dangerous stuff.

After about three years, our Company was converted to Armored Calvary which meant we became a tank unit and began going to Fort Stewart in Georgia. There we were in the woods training but this time we had all of the tanks and other vehicles. At night, I would put my blanket down and sleep in the back of a Personnel Carrier. I didn't have to worry too much at night about snakes, but there were other things we did have to watch out for.

One incident was when a group of us were unloading boxes of flares and could have had a real bad accident or explosion. The flares were coated with wax to protect them from moisture and they were stuck to the bottom of the box. Well this fellow next to me reached in and put his finger through the pin and pulled to break it loose. Just as he started to pull I saw what he was doing and reached over and grabbed my hand around the flare handle just as the pin came out. Holding the handle kept it from going off. It all happened so fast I didn't have time to think, just react. Well, there I was with it in my hand and the other guy with the pin. Somebody yelled to our Lieutenant and he rushed over and had us put tape around the flare, telling me the whole time don't let it go, don't let it go. He had some guys dig a hole and we buried it. In hind sight, we should have just put the pin back in but in all the commotion I'm not sure if the guy still had the pin. You know, I should have received an accommodation for my quick thinking but the Lieutenant never mentioned what happened. It may have reflected badly on him if he had.

When we came in from the field, I would be in classes most of the time studying radio and learning to operate the crypto machine (a machine we used to send encrypted messages). Kay was good about writing letters to me and would always draw cartoons on the envelopes about the things I told her was going on. I really enjoyed getting those letters, and everybody wanted to see the drawings.

I was in the guard for seven years which was all the time I was required to serve. I was just finishing out my seventh year when the First Sergeant brought me some papers to sign. When I asked what they were for he told me they were for reenlistment so I asked "How long do I have to serve?" When he said seven years I said thank you, but no thanks.

Me on Guard Duty
in Rock Hill, S.C.

Kay at 20 years old

In November of 1960, while living in the house on Caruthers Avenue, our middle child LaDonna was born. At the time, the room on the right end was a screened-in porch where LaDonna would spend time crawling around on a blanket as a little one.

Caruthers Avenue

State Street

In the summer of 1961, the owners came back to town and we had to vacate their house so we moved to a small house on State Street. While living on State Street I left Celanese and started my own cabinet business using a contractor's shop and his equipment. The contractor knew I wanted to get in the cabinet business and offered me the use of his shop. I already had an order for a set of kitchen cabinets so I began building them and borrowing the contractor's truck to get the material.

It was then I decided to just build my own truck. I called my old friend Jerry Turner who had an old 1940 Ford he said I could have. We got a cutting torch and cut the body off right behind the front seat. The only thing left from the front seat to the rear bumper was the frame. We then put in a piece of plywood behind the front seat, cut a rectangular hole in it and put in a piece of glass. Now I could see to back up. We then went to a welding shop, taking two coil springs that I had scrounged up from somewhere, and had the springs welded between the frame and the rear axle. Back at the shop, I began work building a wooden body with side rails so I would have me a truck. Luckily, I had the body completed about the same time the cabinets were done.

I continued to pick up work through the winter but unfortunately the old truck didn't last long. In the spring of 1962 I was heading towards Rock Hill from Leslie (an area east of Rock Hill) when the motor started sounding funny. I was coming up to a store called Glasscock's so I pulled in under a big oak tree and stopped. I got out and lifted the hood and discovered the motor had thrown a rod. That meant it was not going anywhere and to get it going meant it would need another motor. I just left it there and had Kay come and pick me up. Looking back, I feel bad about leaving the truck there because Jerry had let me have the old car. I never even paid him a dime for it but then again, he was my best friend.

Redemption & Back to Morgan

That Saturday I was home when two men knocked on the door. It was Jim Moore and Henry Wright, the two men I had worked with at Morgan Fixture Company. They told me that since I had left, three years earlier, Morgan had gone bankrupt and had been purchased by a man from Florida named Joe Jenné. They said Mr. Jenné was trying to find draftsmen so he could get the place opened again and they had told him about me. This man sent them to find me and since we had moved several times, they had spent most of the day tracking me down. They asked if I could come to Charlotte Monday night and meet with them and Mr. Jenné so I did and he offered me a job in the drafting room. At last things were getting better. He explained that he had recently bought Stovall Fixture Company located in Tampa, Florida and was now expanding to Charlotte. He was in need of people in the drafting room, which was exactly what I had wanted to do three years earlier.

God was working in my life.

After going to work for Jenné, we moved to Finley Road in Rock Hill in the summer of 1962. Jeanne de, our youngest child, would be born while we lived there. Things began to get a little better financially and I even bought another car so I could get to Charlotte and back each day.

Work at Jenné went along very well. I was holding my own in the drafting room and my skills continued to improve. Jenné was planning to build a new state of the art fixture plant that would be air conditioned. It was one of the first fixture companies to do so. I really liked the Manager that Jenné had running the place. His name was Richard Bailey, but we all called him Dick. Each time I felt that I should get an increase in pay he would give it to me before I could even ask. He was that in tune with what was going on, not just with business but with the people too.

Finley Road
The fifth place we lived in Rock Hill

Finley Road
A playhouse I built for the girls

I believe it was late 1962 when Kay and I started thinking about building a house one day. With our bad experience in Charlotte, we did not give a thought to moving there again. We knew we wanted to stay in or near Rock Hill. Kay had heard about a new subdivision on the northwest side of Rock Hill called Cedar Forest Acres. So, one Saturday we went out to look at it and found that a road had not been cut into the place yet. We went into it anyway and saw it had been staked with ribbon showing where the different lots and

126

roads would be. We checked it over and picked out two lots. One was on a corner where two roads were planned to intersect and the other piece of property was up the road on an elevated lot.

We had grand dreams as most young people have and were thrilled we would be building a nice new home one day. We let the real estate agent know which two lots we wanted and began making payments of about $30.00 per month. I don't remember what the lots actually cost. We just figured as long as we could make our payments, one day we could start a house. Like most young people though, it wasn't long before we began to miss making our payments. Every so often we would make one, but there came a time when we asked Kay's father if he could make one or two payments for us. After that, not many more payments were made. After a while we almost forgot about the property, thinking that we probably lost it due to lack of payments.

We continued to live at Finley Road as I commuted to Charlotte every day to work. By this time Jenné had completed his new plant in Charlotte and changed the name to Jenné Fixture Company. Jenné had a contract to remodel the Cane Slone Department Store in Nashville, Tennessee so I was sent there with a fellow named Henry Lackey. Henry was the Assistant Manager at the plant and worked in the drafting room. For the job in Nashville, Henry would supervise the work while my job was to draw up the changes and send them back to the plant to be constructed. I did this one area at a time. We were there for about six weeks, part of December and several weeks in January. There was snow on the ground and it was cold as could be.

A lot of the work we received was rush work. The stores did not want areas in the store closed any longer than necessary. I remember one time talking with Henry about the guys in the shop and how hard they worked to meet many of the deadlines. I suggested that we should thank them to show our appreciation for their extra effort. You know what he said? "We show our appreciation on payday." I have never forgotten that and put that knowledge to good use later in life when I began to supervise people. Anyway, Henry and I made it back to Charlotte in late January. I was so glad to be home. Since Kay and I had been married, I had never been gone more than two days before this, other than National Guard camp.

In March of 1963, the plant in Tampa, Florida needed some help in the drafting room so I was sent down to give them a hand. Kay was pregnant with Jeanne de at the time but they allowed me to take the family so Kay and I packed up our stuff along with our two girls, Sammie Kay and LaDonna, and headed for Tampa in our 1958 Chevrolet. We had all our clothes packed in a large wooden crate and shipped by freight to the Fixture plant so it would be there waiting for us.

We drove straight through, about twelve hours. When we arrived one of the Managers from Stovall took us around to find a house we could rent. As I recall we found a small furnished four room house and moved in. During the time we were there, Kay's sister Debra even came down on the bus to visit. There is a scene in our home movies of Debra and us at the beach. While we were there we spent lots of time at the beach and LaDonna in particular got as brown as the locals. I think we were in Florida until May then we came home. Since we were going to make another marathon drive, I cut a piece of plywood and placed it in the back seat tight up to the front seat and covered it with blankets for the kids to sleep on. I drove all the way back, twelve straight hours while Kay kept a hand towel wet so I could stay refreshed until we could get home. What a trip.

I continued to work for Jenné and did some Saturday work for Williams' Cabinet Shop in Rock Hill as well. I remember getting Mr. Williams very concerned one Saturday when he had a big job that had a lot of items just alike. Working at Jenné I was used to listing all the pieces for things and exactly what size to cut them. Mr. Williams had a large stack of plywood and I was just cutting them into various pieces when he came in. He stopped, looked at me and said, "I sure hope you know what you are doing." I did and everything worked out just fine.

Looking for Another Job

In 1964 Belk Department Stores corporate office advertised for store planners so I checked into it and found that Belk was setting up an Architectural and Store Planning Department. This was the time when businesses were moving out of downtown areas and into shopping centers and malls. Belk was gearing up so they could do their own planning instead of hiring private consultants, which could get pricey.

I applied for the job but a friend of mine at Jenné, Carlyle Smith, had also applied. He got the job and I was really down because it made me feel like I was not good enough for the job. I had always felt that Carlyle was better at drawing than I was. So I started to try and think of something else.

A Department Store in Charlotte called Ivey's was a real nice store and one step above Belk. The owner was J.B. Ivey and he had a son J.B. Ivey, Jr. The Ivey's had four stores in the Charlotte area and Jenné did a lot of work for them. J.B., Jr. was always coming into Jenné's to check on their work so I began to plan how I might approach him to ask for a job. I envisioned myself as his assistant looking after his store planning but I never did get a chance to talk with him.

Time went by and I continued to check on other jobs. One Saturday about a year later, I went to check on a job in Anderson, South Carolina. Essex Wire Corporation had a plant there that made electric blanket controls and they were looking for a draftsman. I drove all the way down in a rain storm one Saturday and met with the head Engineer but I learned real quick that he would do the design and I would simply draw it up. I was very disappointed and returned home in a down mood. When I went into work on Monday a friend of mine Jim Moore (yes he was one of the guy's that came and found me in Rock Hill) was now working in the drafting room as well. He knew I was looking for another job and asked me how things were going. I told him it wasn't for me. He asked what I was going to do and I told him I was just going to stay where I was and quit looking. It is interesting how when you quit trying to do things yourself and leave it up to God how things work out. At lunch time, the day I gave up trying to make something happen on my own, the phone rang.

When I answered the phone a man said, "This is Roy Trammel, do you remember me?" It had been about a year since my application at Belk and this is the guy I had applied with. I told him yes I remembered him and then he asked if I would like to talk to him. Of course I said yes. He asked what time I got off work and told me to come by that afternoon. Since he was calling me at work he was very careful that no one knew he was offering me a job at my place of employment. Things were like that back then.

An interesting point I wish to make here, which will repeat all through my life, is how God has played a part in it. Here I was at Jenné Fixture Company looking for a better job. When I gave up and said to Jim I was going to quit looking and quit trying to make something happen, it was like when you ask God to take care of your needs but instead you try to do it. Even though I had not asked God directly for help, he did make things happen when I got out of the way.

When I went for my interview it was with Roy and the head architect, Jean Surratt. Jean was in charge of the architectural division and Roy was in charge of store planning which was what I was being considered for. Lots of questions were asked and I knew what the answers should be. They asked if I had ever flown, meaning on an airplane. I had never been on an airplane in my life but I knew the answer should be yes. Then they asked if it was commercial. At that point in my life I did not even know what they meant by commercial but I knew the answer should be yes.

I went home that day a very excited person feeling, just maybe, that this was going to be my next move. When I got home and told Kay she was very pleased.

Belk & Back to Charlotte

They had me investigated before they offered me the job. We found out from neighbors that someone had been asking a lot of questions about me. I guess they received a good report because in October of 1964 I was hired and began working for Belk Store Services on 5th Street in Charlotte, North Carolina which was the corporate headquarters for Belk and Leggett Department Stores. I left my job with Jenné and began the daily commute from Rock Hill to Charlotte.

After working for Belk Store Services for awhile I told Roy Trammel how I had felt when Carlyle was hired a year before me. He told me at that time they wanted me, but I was making more money than Carlyle so they hired him figuring they would get me later. This sure made me feel better about myself however I still had great respect for Carlyle's ability.

Shortly after going to work at Belk, I was asked to do a survey of an area of a store in Winchester, Virginia. This particular store was a Leggett Store, a Belk Partner, with Leggett owning eighty percent and Belk owning twenty percent. I will explain more about the Belk/Leggett organization later. I was going to Winchester because Leggett had requested to make some changes in the housewares department. Belk offered this service as part of their agreement so plans were made for me to go, airline tickets were bought, and arrangements made for a rental car and hotel room.

Remember now I had never been on an airplane in my life. On the day I was supposed to leave I took the ticket information and headed to the airport. At least I knew how to get there; I had always been good at reading a map. However, when I walked in the airport I had no idea where to go and I didn't know what airline I was supposed to take. So I just walked up to the first counter and handed the ticket to them. They looked at it and pointed me over to the proper airline where they took care of everything. I got on the plane and when I arrived at Washington National Airport, I found the car rental place and they gave me a map to Winchester. I knew I could do this.

No one at Belk must have checked on what was happening in Winchester. The entire town was having the Apple Blossom Festival and parade so the store was closing at noon. The manager went home to change clothes and bring his family back to watch the parade and locked me in the store so I could get my work done while he was gone. When he returned, we put some stools in the show window and watched the parade together. The next day I finished up my work and went home. Not only had my first experience on an airplane been a success, but after I wrote up and submitted my report, I was complimented on doing such a nice job.

I continued at Belk Store Services doing work on many of the Belk stores. There were numerous partners in the company and at one time or another I worked on all of their stores. In fact, there were Belk and Leggett stores all up and down the East Coast. One day Roy Trammel called me into his office and proceeded to tell me, "If I was after his job he would chew me up and spit me out." His exact words as I recall. Well I was flabbergasted at this! All I was trying to do was a good job at whatever was asked of me. I never did find out what prompted Roy to say that to me.

One day after I had been at Belk for a while, I was sitting at my drawing board working on a store. I was drawing everything in real neat when Roy came up and looked at what I was doing. He did not make any comments, he just picked up a pencil and marked all over what I was doing. This made me mad and he noticed. Then he explained this was supposed to be a work sheet, not a finished drawing. His point was well taken and I began to learn to roughly sketch everything in first, such as establishing department areas and traffic aisles before putting in individual fixtures. I didn't like how Roy went about correcting me that day, but I never forgot what he told me about doing a rough sketch first.

Although Kay, her family and our children had always been close, I began to feel that my future would be in Charlotte or somewhere else and thought this would be a good time to move closer to my job and make a break from her family. So, in the spring of 1968, we moved again to Charlotte, initially looking for a house to rent but ended up buying one instead. By this time all the kids were in school and Kay got a job at a photo lab in Charlotte to help with our income.

Like I said, our intention was to rent a house not to buy one. What happened was that I went to a Real Estate company looking for a house to rent, but the lady took me to see two new houses next to each other and tried to get me interested in buying one of them. The house was only 1,000 sq. ft. but I told her I had no down payment and could not afford to buy a house. She asked if she could work it out would I consider buying this house. I said yes as long as my payments were no more than $100.00 a month because that was all we could afford. So here's what she did. She had me go to the bank and put my first month's rent in a savings account in my name and bring the book to her. She told us we could go ahead and move in and on the first of each month to come get the book and make my $100.00 deposit and return the book to her, so I did. After we had $600.00 in the savings account, we made a withdrawal and used that money as a down payment to buy the house on Winedale Lane; we paid $12,000 for it. There we were with no money but were allowed to move in and live in the house free for six months which enabled us to save the down payment. I felt that God was looking after us again.

In 1969 I decided to make sure I kept our house bug free so I bought some bug spray and crawled under the house. Interestingly, while I was under the house, I found a "V" nickel lying right on top of the dirt. Remember, five had always been my lucky number. Then again, after sharing with you the rest of what happened, maybe five wasn't so lucky for me on that occasion. You see, a few days later I was at work and suddenly my heart just started to race. I passed out and came too still sitting at my drawing board. Later I found out I had fallen to the floor and was picked up and put back in my

Winedale Lane in Charlotte, N.C.

chair. The rescue squad took me to my doctor where he examined me and said it was my nerves. I had never had any issues like this before. The Doctor did not ask and I did not think to connect it to the spray.

I continued with problems and could not stand being in a crowd of people and began to have a hurting feeling in my throat. It felt like a lump and every time I swallowed it hurt. I began to pray on my way to work and on my way home asking God to heal me but nothing happened. This went on for weeks with me continuing to ask for healing. I would quote scripture, ask and you shall receive, ask in Jesus name and on and on. One day on the way home I got real frustrated and said to God, "I have been asking for healing and nothing is happening. I don't believe you can do it. If you can do it, let's see you do it." Precisely, at that moment the lump in my throat began to move. It went at a slow pace straight up and out the top of my head. I was stopped at a traffic light, a horn blew, and I made my right turn and pulled off the road. The lump was gone, I swallowed several times, and it was gone, truly gone. I was amazed and drove on home, about ten minutes, but by the time I got home I could feel the lump coming back. However, over the next week it slowly went away.

All my life I had trouble believing and had asked for God's help many times so finally I told him that I needed him to kick me in the ass. I really did. Well, this day I got my ass kicked. I told my Dad about it and he said, "Oh you should not have done that," saying what I did to God. I told my Minister and he said "Well you asked God to heal you and he did," but I told him "No, I asked God to heal me and he did not. It was only when I said "I don't believe you can do it" that he healed me."

If I had been healed when I asked for healing I could have explained it away as the power of positive thinking or mind over matter, etc. Happening the way it did, in a negative fashion I cannot explain it any other way other than God did it. I know now without a doubt that there is a God. I will never forget what happened to me in Charlotte that day. It has completely changed my outlook on life. By the way, it turned out that the bug spray I used, Chlordane, was a nerve agent and was taken off the market some time later.

We continued living in the house on Winedale Lane where our three girls had many friends to play with and I became "Mr. Fixit" man with all the kids' bicycles. We even had a special project one time where I asked them to bring home any parts of bicycles they could find and we would make one from scratch. So, they began to bring me all kinds of parts from bikes and exercise machines, etc. One day they gathered around and we put all the things together to make a bicycle so they could ride it. These were the kinds of adventures with the kids we all enjoyed.

Another adventure was after Kay had decided to become a Girl Scout leader. We have lots of fond memories of working with the Girl Scouts on cookouts and camping trips and making a huge Halloween "scare tent" from black plastic. One time we took the Girl Scouts to the mountains for a Girl Scout Jamboree. We set up our tents in a little valley running up towards the mountain. Kay and I and the other adults had big tents on one side and all the girls set up in front of us on the other side, about fifty yards away. We had all settled in for the night when it began to rain, but it didn't just rain, it poured! It wasn't long before our troop of girls came running to our tent because their pup-tents were leaking. Before you knew it, we had all the kids in our tent and even though we were packed, we made it through the night. What an experience.

Girl Scouts

The three girls at Tweetsy
Railroad in N.C.

Girl Scout camping

I continued with Belk working on many different stores. In fact, Belk had many partners which they had teamed up with as Belk expanded. Rather than run someone out of business they would partner with the local store owner offering bulk buying. Everyone usually accepted the arrangement. In most cases, Belk would own fifty-one percent, which gave them controlling interest and put their name first such as "Belk Berry," "Belk Lindsey" or "Belk Parks" and others. One of their partners was Leggett Stores in the edge of North Carolina, and while most of the stores were in Virginia, there were some in Maryland, Delaware and West Virginia. At their peak, Leggett had sixty-five stores.

The Leggett brothers used to work for Belk in Mathews, North Carolina then they left and started their own stores in Virginia, first in South Boston, and then in

Lynchburg. After they had been operating for a while, Belk asked about coming on board and doing a buy-in. Leggett agreed and sold them twenty percent. With Belk having only twenty percent, Leggett retained the right to run the stores without Belk input or interference. Belk wanted to open stores in Danville, Virginia and the Raleigh/Durham N.C. area. Eventually they did and the stores were opened with Belk having a controlling interest of fifty-one percent. As other stores were opened, Leggett held control at eighty percent.

While living on Winedale Lane, I bought a pop up camper. Me, Kay and the three girls would go camping and have all kinds of different camping adventures. I even made a rack for the top of the camper so we could put five bicycles up there. At Myrtle Beach we would set up at the campground and would ride our bicycles everywhere we went. We made many trips and had great times together as a family.

In 1969, I decided that my Dad, my brothers and I should use the camper and take a hunting trip back to Shulerville where we came from. We made the trip and when we got there, we camped way back in the woods and hunted hogs for two days. We had very good luck killing three hogs, but these were not wild boars but hogs that had been loose in the woods for so long, they really were wild. We had a great time being together and talking about the past. That was the last time we hunted together as a group.

Dad   Lester

Furman on the   Mendel   Hogs
right

My work at Belk included many stores such as "Belk Berry," in North Carolina, "Belk Hudson" in South Carolina, and "Belk Lindsey" in Florida. One particular partner I enjoyed working for was Mr. E.O. Hudson in Spartanburg, South Carolina. This Hudson was not related to the Hudson's in the Raleigh/Durham area of North Carolina. I worked mostly with his son E.O., Jr. and it was particularly nice when he bought a drawing board and set it up near his office so when I would come down we could sit there and plan the store together. E.O., Jr. enjoyed sitting there watching me work. I also had numerous comments and praises from Belk partners and store managers regarding the quality of my work.

I remember going to Franklin, Virginia and meeting with the store manager, Mr. Blair. When I was ready to leave, he walked up and handed me a box and thanked me for coming. I thanked him for the gift and left. In the car I opened the box and saw he had given me a shirt. Back at the office I was telling the story to the people I worked with and showed them the shirt then put the box on the shelf above my drawing board. That evening I took the box home and showed the shirt to Kay. When she took the shirt out, there in the box under the shirt was a pair of large red panties. These things were a size fifty-two with a note attached that read, "In remembrance of me – Brenda Sue." I immediately knew someone at the office had played a trick on me. I figured it had to be John Furr but when I asked him he denied it. I asked everyone and no one would admit it. Years later I asked John and he still said he didn't do it. However, I kept those panties and they turned up again later in my life. Keep reading, you will see.

Destiny

In 1968, I was on a business trip to Georgia and after getting off the plane and renting a car, I headed for the store in Valdosta about twenty-five miles away. I knew exactly how to get there because I had been there several times before. Well, I got to an intersection where I was supposed to go straight across, but for some reason I made a right turn on this four lane highway. I was cruising along and suddenly I realized what I had done. I pulled over, looked at the map and saw a road to the left that would take me at an angle back to the road I missed. I made the left turn and about five miles down the road I saw a women on the left side waving at me with a child in her arms. I knew she was in trouble so I slammed on the brakes so hard that the car choked down. I got it restarted, turned around, and went back to where she was.

I got out and asked what was wrong. She said something about her child and I could tell he wasn't breathing. I did not know what to do except try mouth-to-mouth resuscitation to revive the child, so I did. I put the two of them in the car and told the mother to continue doing mouth-to-mouth. I asked her where her husband worked and she said at a saw mill back up the road from where I had come. We took off and stopped at the saw mill, picked up her husband, and headed for the hospital which happened to be back to the four lane highway and left about ten miles. I was driving at least seventy or eighty miles per hour and I don't even remember if cars had emergency blinkers back then. Suddenly a trooper came around me and motioned for me to follow him. He led me to the hospital and they took over.

I found out what was wrong. The child had died of something that was very contagious which startled me because I had tried to resuscitate him. The doctor gave me medicine to take, which I started immediately but I felt so bad for the parents. This must have been their only child. I went to them and told them how sorry I was for their loss.

They thanked me for what I had done and then I left. I went back and took the same road to where I had seen her in the yard. As I went by I began to think that if I had not made my wrong turn she would still be there waiting for help. This was a lonely stretch of road and I don't remember seeing any other houses or cars until I got back on the road I should have been on to start with. I began to realize that I had been led to be where I was supposed to be to offer her some help. Many such things have happened before that made me realize, God is working in my life.

Time went on and one day J.B. Ivey, Jr. came in because the Belk's were showing him around. I began to think again of going to work for him and would think about all kind of ways to approach the matter. In the meantime, I began doing some work for the Leggett stores. At that time the five Leggett sons, Gordon, Bill, Bobby, Tommy and Fred, were managers and also known as the Fixture Committee.

After a couple of jobs they began to ask that I do the next one and so it went until I was the one doing all of their work. We would meet in Charlotte at Belk headquarters in the big conference room. We needed the big room because of all the people involved which consisted of the five young Leggett's, Mr. Harold Leggett of the first generation, the store Manager, and sometimes Mr. Robert Leggett, Sr. would be there as well. Things would get pretty loud because they were constantly changing things. Someone would get their way one day and somebody else another day. After these planning sessions, some of my fellow store planners would remark, "I would not want to put up with all that." But I kept plugging along. We finally began meeting in Lynchburg, Virginia and usually Jerry Kistler from our office went with me. I would work with the Leggett's making a rough sketch of an area then give it to Jerry to draw to scale.

One day when we broke for lunch, everyone started off down the street while Jerry and I washed up because our hands were dirty from all the drawing. After we cleaned up, Gordon Leggett was waiting for us and as we walked down the street he said to me, "You know Sam, we just don't seem to be making much progress" and asked what we might do about it. Well I had been thinking about this and told him I thought there were too many people involved. If I had one person to work with things would go smoother. Within several weeks the Fixture Committee was disbanded. Gordon became Human Resource Manager, Bill took Real Estate and Store Development, Bobby took over Finance and Control, Tommy was in charge of Merchandising, and Fred became head of Transportation and Communication (transportation because the company had an airplane). I should point out that the finances were actually handled in Lynchburg by Mr. Epes, then later by Mr. Marion Mason. Bobby's title was in name only.

With this change, all of my work would be with Bill Leggett. He would come to Charlotte and we would go over how the store should be laid out, the location of aisles and the various departments. Remember now, I was still thinking about how I could go to work for J.B. Ivey when one day I thought, "What am I doing? Ivey has four stores and Leggett has sixty-five. I'm looking in the wrong direction!" So from that day forward I set my sights on Leggett. At the time, Belk and Leggett stores were mostly located downtown and parking was beginning to be a real problem. However, shopping centers were opening up around every town and we were opening new stores in the shopping centers and later in the malls. There was a lot going on.

One day after Hurricane Hazel came through I received a call from Bill Leggett asking me to come to Waynesboro, Virginia. The town had flooded and water was three feet deep in the store. He had already cleared it with my boss and had their plane on the way to pick me up. I rushed home, packed a bag and headed for the airport. I was waiting when the plane landed and we headed for Waynesboro. By this time I had met and gotten to know both of the pilots. As we neared Waynesboro they dropped down low so we could see the areas that had the worst flooding. Just before we reached Charlottesville, Virginia along Route 29, we could see where a number of houses had been washed away and had already heard that some people had been lost in the devastation. In some places, water was still rushing across the road.

When we arrived in Waynesboro there were motor boats in the streets. The low end of the town was flooded, which happened to be where the store was located. Most of the water had receded around the store though so merchandise was being brought out to the parking lot. I immediately got busy getting counters and racks from the store so they would have a place to put everything. This store did have a second floor and as much merchandise as possible had already been carried up there out of the flood waters. The employees were also busy sorting through clothes to be sent to the laundry. With the flooding, sewer systems had backed up so the water was contaminated. Everything had to be washed first before it could be sold. We worked into the night and were ready for the big flood sale the next day. After the sale, we washed down the damaged fixtures and put them in the parking lot and sold them as well. Some things we just gave away so we would not have to bother taking them to the dump. At the end of the day we measured the high water mark at forty-two inches in the store.

Then the cleanup began. I had to take inventory of all damaged fixtures including showcases so our loss could be submitted to the insurance company. I was also busy ordering new furniture and fixtures, carpeting and everything that would be needed to fit out the first floor for business. Thankfully we were able to call on one of our suppliers, Stanley Fixture Company who got to work making everything we needed. Before the fixtures arrived, we had the new carpet down and ready to restock the first floor. Throughout this entire process the second floor was open for business while we were refurnishing the first floor.

A New Plan Develops

Back in Charlotte it was business as usual. When Bill Leggett would come down he had to meet with the legal department about leases, the architectural department about building design, and with me on interior layout. He was quite busy. I began to think and plan how to approach him on what I had been thinking about. One day while he was sitting at my drawing board I said to him, "You know Bill, when you are down here you have so much to check on, legal architectural and everything else, that we have little time to plan the layout. I think we could get a lot more done if I was in Charlottesville with you." Well he turned and looked at me and said, "That's the craziest damn thing I ever heard." I did not say another word.

That afternoon when we left to go home Bob Bramhall, who now had Roy Trammel's job (Roy had left to open his own planning office and took Carlyle Smith with him) said that Bill had asked him and Jean Surratt as he was leaving if I could come to Charlottesville and work up there. Of course what he was thinking was Belk would pay my salary. Several weeks later Leggett Stores decided that they would pay my salary and approached John Belk, the President of Belk stores, about the possibility of me transferring to Leggett. Of course John said no because he did not want to have the stores starting their own thing, plus he certainly didn't want any of his planners leaving. When I found out the problem I called Bill and asked him what was going own.

He said that John did not want me to go. I got upset that John was interfering with what I saw as advancement for me so I asked Bill, "Do you want me to come to work for you?" He said yes, so I asked "If I was not working for Belk tomorrow would you hire me?" He said no he could not do that without John's blessing. I then went to see Bob Bramhall and told him I wanted to have a meeting with John Belk. Bob said to let him see what he could do. I told him that the way I saw it, Leggett wanted to hire me, I wanted the job and I felt

145

John had no right to hold me back. In fact, I felt that it was illegal for him to do so. I then said to Bob, you tell Mr. Belk that either I get the job or I quit and so either way I would not be working for Belk.

Months passed, then one day a call came in and the secretary announced over the speaker a phone call for Bob Bramhall from Bill Leggett. When I heard this I knew it was about me. I knew this because every time Bill called it was always for me. Shortly after that, Bill called me and told me everything had been worked out and asked if I could come to Charlottesville, Virginia with Kay to discuss everything. This was September of 1970. To say the least, I was thrilled.

I found out later that Mr. Harold Leggett was involved in John changing his mind. The story goes like this. A year earlier Bill's father Mr. Harold was very sick, so the whole thing about me was put on hold. Once he was back in better health, the Leggett's were having a meeting. At some point Mr. Harold asked how things were coming along as far as me coming to Charlottesville to help Bill. Bill explained the problem with John Belk not wanting to let me go. At this point Mr. Harold picked up the phone and called John, they had a little talk and things got worked out, thank God.

John Belk had said OK, so Kay and I made our plans, bought our airline tickets, took the kids to Grandma's and flew into Richmond, Virginia. There we rented a car and drove west to Charlottesville. Interstate 64 had not been built yet so we took highway 250 which brought us into Charlottesville at an area called Pantop's Mountain. As you crested the top of the hill, as it was not really a mountain, spread out below was the lights of the city or at least half of it. It was beautiful and located at the foothills of the Blue Ridge Mountains. It was a lot like going back to Rock Hill because it had that small town flavor. We fell in love with it. Why not, I had a new job with great future potential, was working directly with one of the second generation Leggett's, and for a company that had sixty-five department stores.

Kay and I met with Bill Leggett the next morning. I introduced him to Kay and he showed us around the store and then we settled down to talk business. We talked about my responsibilities and the fact that I would have a company

146

car at my disposal 24/7. We talked salary and their profit sharing program. I was at a disadvantage though since he already had all that information from Belk. Although his offer was about what I was making with Belk, the future with Leggett I felt would be better.

Bill had a real estate agent lined up to show us around so Kay and I met with the agent and told him the price range we were looking for. Something around $20,000 dollars is what we felt we could afford. The agent took us to an area just around the corner from houses that were selling in the $50,000 range. The house he showed us was a split foyer, around 1,400 sq. ft. with a full unfinished basement on a cul-de-sac. The price was $29,900. I could see no way we could afford this and told him so. I asked him to show us something around $20,000.

He took us to another area where some modular homes were being built. These houses were manufactured and brought to the site in two pieces and they certainly looked like it. You could see where they were joined together on the outside ends and the insides weren't much better. We were very disappointed, so he continued to show us a number of places in and out of town. We spent that night wondering what in the world we were going to do.

The next day we met again with the agent and ended up with the first house he had showed us, the one on the cul-de-sac. I think Mr. Leggett had told the agent the area or the quality of house we should have. With this house at $29,900 our payments would be around $200 a month, which meant that Kay would probably have to go to work.

It was September of 1970 and we were preparing to move to Charlottesville. We went back to Charlotte and set everything in motion. First, we put our house up for sale through the realtor we had purchased it from. Then I went to the realtor in Rock Hill that we had bought the two lots from in Cedar Forest Acres. I told him we were moving and we needed to sell the lots. He took the price we bought them for and the price they were currently selling at, less what we had paid on them, and wrote us a check for the difference. Is that not good or what?

The house in Charlotte ended up selling for $15,500 which was $3,500 dollar profit for us. This $3,500, the money we received from the lots and a little money Kay had saved up was exactly what we needed for the down payment on the house in Charlottesville. Somebody was really looking out for us.

Our house in Charlottesville, Virginia
I built the curved brick wall

After the moving company left with our belongings we loaded up and headed out. I was driving the 1958 Chevrolet with Sammie Kay, our oldest daughter, and Kay was driving the Buick that we had bought new earlier that year. She had LaDonna and Jeanne de with her. She was also pulling the camper which we were going to spend the night in when we got to Charlottesville. It was late when we reached Danville, Virginia but about half way through the city the police pulled me over. Kay saw what had happened and pulled in behind me. What a welcome to Virginia this was going to be! It turned out okay though. Apparently the police pulled me over because they saw I had a very young girl in the car and it was late at night. Sammie Kay was eleven at the time. After explaining our circumstances they wished us a safe trip and on we went. We spent our first night in Charlottesville in the camper at a campground.

The next day the moving company arrived, and we moved into our new home and got settled. Remember I said there was an unfinished basement? Well, we had the building contractor put in a master bedroom on one side of the basement for Kay and me. There was already plumbing installed for a bathroom down there and another large area with a fire place, perfect for a family room. I knew I could finish off these spaces myself without a problem and did that during the next year. We got the girls into school, I began my new job, and Kay got a job at a bank as a teller at the drive through (because she was so pretty I think). Over time, we slowly began to make new friends.

I had no office at work so I set up in the hallway near the customer service area. There was a set of women's toilets and lounge on the second floor that had been closed earlier. Bill had been using the lounge as his office so I set out to redo the toilet area for my office. Two weeks later I moved into the women's toilet. A heck of a way to start, but it worked out just fine. We put a desk in the foyer in front of the toilets and hired a secretary. Now I could go to work.

Early 1970's
Back Row Left to Right: LaDonna, Jeanne de, Sammie Kay
Front Row: Me and Kay

Settling in Charlottesville

Kay was driving the Buick and I was using the 1958 Chevrolet and since this was September, I had to get the cars inspected and get Virginia tags. The Buick was not a problem but the Chevrolet was. It needed three or four hundred dollars worth of work and since the guy that worked at the garage wanted to buy it, I sold the Chevrolet to him. So far, I had not heard anything about my promised company car.

I went to Bill and told him we had a problem. He asked what it was and I said I didn't have a car to drive. I then explained about the work mine needed and that I had sold it and would need my company car. You could tell he didn't like the box I had put him into, but he contacted Lynchburg and they found me a used car. I was using it on trips to visit the stores but on every trip I would have to put oil in it. After a few months, I went to Bill and told him I was concerned that it would break down and leave me stranded and I thought they needed to get me a new car. They finally did and things were getting better.

We loved Charlottesville, Virginia. It was like going back to Rock Hill. The few years we lived in Charlotte, North Carolina, we hated it. Charlotte was too big, too congested, and had too much crime. After moving to Charlottesville, our first trip back to Rock Hill was at Christmas. We had a very nice trip and on our return as we came out of Lynchburg, you could see the Blue Ridge Mountains in the distance. I turned to Kay and asked "Do you feel what I feel?" She said "Yes, we are almost home." You know that feeling you get, well we had it in just four months, that's how much we liked where we were.

We went to a New Year's Eve party that year at a Catholic School with some friends we had met. When we were heading over to the party, it was snowing and the ground was already covered. We enjoyed the party and after midnight, they served everyone breakfast. We had a great time and met many new friends. When we went outside the snow had stopped but when I opened the car door it pushed several inches of snow out of the way. I looked at Kay and said, "What have we gotten ourselves into?" I was referring to the weather. The next day I bought a snow blower and a set of tire chains.

My relationship with Bill Leggett was fine but he and I definitely came from different backgrounds. You see, he came up as the son of one of the original founders of Leggett stores and I think he felt he was in a higher class, financially and otherwise, than most people. He was nice and polite to people but there was something there.

One day after I had been there for a while, I was leaving for lunch and saw him at the escalator so I said, "I am going to lunch, would you like to join me?" and he said, "I don't eat with the help." I swear that is what I remember and it really got to me. When I got home that evening I told Kay what had happened. She could not believe it. I remember telling her that if he wanted it that way then fine, from that point forward our relationship would be strictly business. Another time I noticed he and I both had on a green suit and I commented on it. He said no they were not the same, they were the same color. You see, what he was referring to is he bought his from an exclusive men's store next door while I bought my clothes from Leggett. Another time Bill made a clear distinction regarding his job and mine. When I asked about something having to do with Real Estate, Bill remarked that he would handle Real Estate and I should stick to Store Planning.

Other than these few remembrances he and I got along just fine. What happened was that I soon learned my job was working for the stores and the store managers. If I kept them happy by taking care of their needs, then everything was fine. The store managers had to deal with all the other Leggett's including Mr. Harold Leggett, Bill's father, as well as the other founders. It helped that the managers were saying good things about me and letting it be known how good I was at helping them. Mr. Harold really liked me too and when I ran into him he would always ask me, "How is Bill doing?" I always gave a good report. I never said anything negative.

Aside from work and making new friends, we joined First Presbyterian Church. Even though we joined mainly for the girls, we really enjoyed the fellowship. The Pastor, Dr. Bestebreurtje (affectionately called "Dr. B.") was Dutch and had worked in the Dutch underground during World War II. He always preached that God was a God of history, ordinary things happen, but God controls the outcome. We really liked Dr. B.

Unfortunately, Dr. B. was in a tragic accident in January of 1983. He was an accomplished ice skater and used to go to the lake in the winter time with a friend of his and ice skate. On this particular day he was skating out in front of his friend when the ice broke. Dr. B. went in and under the ice. His friend could not save him.

During my early years in Charlottesville I had a lot of trouble with my nerves. This was a result of my exposure to Chlordane when I was in Charlotte. Many times my heart would race and I would head for the doctor. I ended up on a regimen of Shaklee vitamins and over time I improved.

During this same time there was a fellow who had been working for Leggett for many years. His name was Mr. Noel Smith and he primarily looked after the store's buildings. He had a son that worked for Belk in Charlotte when I was there; he was one of their Architects. Even though he was much older than I was, Noel and I got to be real good friends and traveled together some.

Noel shared a story with me about when he was in the Portsmouth store as it was being remodeled. (This was before my time with the company). He said he was looking up at something and took a step or two backwards and fell off the balcony floor, there were no guard rails. Luckily, there was a truck with insulation piled in the back and he landed right on top of the pile and did not get hurt. Well, maybe his pride was hurt. I remember when he lived in Lynchburg, Virginia and invited my whole family down for the weekend.

We all got along well and he really liked our three girls. Noel is buried in Danville, Virginia in a cemetery on 29 North.

Of course, salary adjustments were made at the end of each year but after several years I felt my salary was not where it should be so I asked Bill about it. He seemed annoyed that I brought it up and asked how much I thought I should be making, so I told him what I thought I should be making. His remark was, "You expect to make as much as Mason?" You see, Mr. Mason was the Controller for the company and had just taken over the position from Mr. Epes (who started with the original founders) but had retired. Because of that slip I then knew what Mason was making.

A few weeks later I was in Lynchburg and happened to see Mr. Harold and of course he asked about Bill. Then he said, "How much are we paying you?" I told him and he said, "You should be making and quoted a number." I told him that Bill and I had discussed that amount. He said he had been sick the past year when salaries were discussed but he would be there this year. I thanked him and he said, "Don't you tell Bill that we had this talk." I said I would not and asked him to not mention it either. Bill would have felt that I went around him and talked to his father, which I didn't do. Mr. Harold was the one who had brought it up.

We were always evaluated at the first of the year after Christmas because the stores did most of their business during Christmas. So, by January we knew what kind of year we had as a company. The manager's pay checks were mailed to their homes and since I was in management, mine was too. Usually after you received your increase you would naturally go to your boss and thank him for whatever increase you received. I got my check and noticed I had my increase, but I did not say anything to Bill. A week and a half went by and one day he asked if I had received my check, to which I said yes I had, and he said, "I hope you are happy, you got what you asked for." I told him I was pleased and I thanked him.

It is said, "Do unto others," so as time went on it became my job to go to Charlotte to give direction to the planners as to how we wanted our store planned. Basically, I was now doing what Bill had been doing when I worked at Belk, except I did not get involved in Real Estate questions. One day at the airport waiting to catch the plane was a number of Leggett people and one of them was Mr. Mason. I handled all the invoices having anything to do with my responsibility and after checking each one I would sign and forward them to him to pay. He and I got along well

Anyway, all the Leggett people had their plane tickets while another Leggett person and I had finished our work a day early and were on standby. When the plane began to load, Mr. Mason wished us luck on getting home. We said thanks and that we would see him later. After they had boarded we went forward and we were told they had available seats, so they marked our tickets and said we could board. When we walked into the plane, you of course go through the first class area but as we started thorough, the stewardess stopped us, looked at our tickets and showed us our seats. They had put us in first class.

As you may know, first class seats are large compared to the seats in coach. I sat there until we had taken off, then I got up and went back to Mr. Mason. You have to understand, Mr. Mason was a very big man and he was squeezed into his seat. I told him we had made it aboard and offered him my seat. He refused it, but thanked me very much. I think this gesture helped me in many ways after that, especially when we had to move to South Boston, Virginia. That will come later in my story.

A PLACE CALLED HELLHOLE SWAMP

156

Hunting Adventures

I slowly began to get interested again in hunting and fishing like I used to do when Kay and I were first married. To begin with, I went by myself because I could only do it when I could fit it in around my work schedule. I bought myself a bow, a long bow, because I had made that type when I was in my teens. I began to practice and would go to an old apple orchard near the Blue Ridge Mountains. I would see deer but I never got a shot. One day I was discussing hunting with someone and he said he had a recurve bow he wanted to sell. The difference between a long bow and a recurve is simply that a long bow is straight and a recurve's tips are bent forward. You can get the same power from the recurve and it is shorter and easier to handle. So I bought it and continued hunting at the apple orchard.

One day I had gone in to hunt at about three in the afternoon. I parked my car and walked up the mountain following the fence that separated the apple trees from the woods. I had my portable tree stand with me because it is much easier to hunt from up in a tree. Deer tend not to look up in trees. They watch the ground because that is where their danger comes from. Well, I found a nice tree right along the fence line and set my stand around the tree.

The type of tree stand I used was called a climbing stand. By that I mean you have a foot piece that hooks around the tree and when you step on it, it pinches on the tree. You have a seat that works the same way. You stand up on the foot piece and raise the seat, then you sit and raise the foot and work your way up the tree. If you encounter limbs you cut them so you can keep going. Usually I liked to be about fifteen feet off the ground.

Well this day in September was warm, so I just turned around with my feet hanging free and sat there to cool down. I did not expect to see anything until closer to dark. In a little while I thought I heard talking, so I listened and sure enough there was talking and it was coming from down the fence line

157

I had just followed. I sat and continued to listen. Then I saw movement. It was two young girls on horseback coming up the trail. I figured I better stand up so they wouldn't see me so I quickly stood up and on they came talking and watching the trail. As they got closer I thought I should say something to let them know I was there but I thought if I say something now it may spook the horses and the girls might get hurt, so I just froze standing with my back against the tree. They walked right on by and never knew I was there.

After they had gone I was so nervous that I sat down again. Within thirty minutes guess what came walking up that same trail, you're right, just what I came to hunt for, a deer. It was a doe which is legal when hunting with a bow, so I sat there wondering how I could shoot sitting down. I couldn't stand up because that would spook the deer. So I thought maybe I can shoot sitting so I got ready, and when she was right under me I pulled the bow back and let the arrow fly. Well, I missed and she ran up the trail but then stopped and turned around because she didn't know what happened. I sat there disgusted and then I saw a little baby with spots coming up the trail following her Mama. I felt really bad and told myself from now on I will only shoot the bucks.

Another day I got back from a trip in the afternoon and went straight to the same place. It was a little later in the afternoon, so I walked in real slow with my bow and arrow ready. About half way up, I saw a buck off to my right run out of the bushes going up the mountain so I stopped and crouched down behind a little rise in front of me. I waited though because deer are very inquisitive. Sure enough, as I waited I could hear his steps over the rise. What he was doing was coming back to see what was coming up the trail. I heard him stop, so I slowly stood up with my bow ready to shoot, he just stood there looking at me so I let the arrow fly. You're right; I missed him and hit a tree. My hunting skills obviously needed some work. Later that afternoon as I walked out, I got in my car and started to leave, I noticed a deer down in a little bottom feeding on honeysuckle. I pulled on past him and quietly got out with my bow and crawled back to where I could shoot. I got up on my knees and let go another arrow.

It hit the ground right under the deer. I was having an adventure but sure wasn't having much success.

I hunted this area a lot but another time I came in and crawled over the fence and went over the next hill. I thought I would wait there and catch the deer when they were leaving the apple orchard. I decided not to use my tree stand that day so I positioned myself next to a big tree on the ground. I stood there perfectly still with my bow at the ready. Within an hour I saw four deer coming from my left down the hill about a hundred yards from me. Oh boy, this is my chance so I got ready. Just then, one of the deer saw me or saw something that did not look right in the woods, so she came to investigate and came to within forty yards, stopped and looked straight at me. Then she picked up one front foot and stomped the ground. I stood still. She stomped again. I never moved. Then she turned and jumped two or three times like she was going to run. Then she stopped and looked back at me. I still did not move, so she just walked on off with the others like I wasn't there. You see, she was trying to get me to move. Since I did not, she must have thought I was part of the tree.

I then walked down a dry stream bed looking for tracks to see where they were crossing going into the apple orchard. I found a place with lots of tracks and knew I had to go farther on because the bucks will always cross or walk a little bit away from the does. About twenty yards down from where the does were, there was one set of tracks. I figured this had to be a buck. I picked out a tree nearby and decided this is where I would put my tree stand the next time I came in. The next time that's what I did. I was in my stand and ready when I saw three does coming down the left side of the dry stream bed. They came straight to where they had crossed before and crossed over again. I looked behind them and here came the buck just as I figured. He walked to the place I had scouted and crossed and then he stopped and looked around. I was ready with my bow; he was not that far from the tree I was in. So I took carful aim and released my arrow. Thump, it went just over his back. Shooting down at that steep angle caused my aim to be off. He ran off about forty yards and stopped. I nocked another arrow and fired again this time hitting the ground at his feet. Something has to change, I thought. I determined I might have to use a gun. I sure wasn't having much luck with my bow.

I decided to try another place where I had permission to hunt so one Saturday morning before daylight I arrived at the place, got my bow and headed into the woods. This place I had never been before so I went in very slowly and walked up to the top of a rise that looked to be fairly open, so I decided this would be a good place. I looked around and saw a holly tree that had limbs all the way down to the ground. I figured I could cut some limbs and snuggle into the opening and would be hidden pretty well.

So I leaned my bow against one of the limbs and began to cut away the others. When I cut the last limb my knife went through the limb and hit the bow string. "Twang" I heard and thought "oh crap I cut the bow string." I checked my pocket for the extra string I usually carried but realized it was in the trunk of my car. So I looked all around and finally found the short piece of my bow string; the long piece was still on the bow. Now what am I going to do? I decided maybe I could tie them together. Do you know how many strings are in a bow string? Eight as I recall. How do you tie eight strings that have wax on them? Well, I will tell you what I did. First I thought I might tie the whole thing in a knot but it slipped right loose. Then I tried to tie each of the eight strings but that didn't work so I decided I would have to tie the ends of the strings back on itself, then tie each of the other strings through the first ones, then back on themselves to make it work.

Now to accomplish this I was down on the ground with my flashlight shining on what I was working on and I hear a deer snort, then he came charging straight at me. It was dark and I couldn't see a thing. I turned the light off real quick and said to myself, you best get this thing ready to shoot. So I turned the light back on and continued to tie the strings while he charged again. By the time I finished, he was gone. I must have walked in and gotten between him and a doe and since this was mating season he couldn't make out what that was huddled down on the ground between him and his girl. In hindsight I could have been killed. I won't do that again.

I always had different hunting spots I would visit. In fact, a couple of friends and I would go to Quantico Marine Base each year to deer hunt. You see, we knew the Base Game Warden because his wife worked for Leggett Department Store in Fredericksburg, Virginia and through her we were able to go up, have the Game Warden issue our permits and assign us to an area to hunt. To hunt on the base you were supposed to go there ahead of time and take a study course and then put your name in for a drawing to determine whether you got a spot or not. We didn't have to do that. Anyway, after we had received our passes, we would go to our designated area and scatter while each of us would find a place and sit down. After daylight we would begin to move looking for deer and checking for a good place to come to the next day. Somehow we would get a deer each year.

One year on the first day of the hunt daylight broke and I began to move looking for a good spot for the next day. It was then I saw a tree stand built against a big oak tree so I quietly climbed up. On the top step there were a number of notches. It is common practice for hunters to make a notch for each kill so I thought this has got to be a good place. I settled myself in, standing and leaning against the tree. I was up there for an hour before I saw any movement and what I saw was a doe coming straight for the tree I was in. When she got there she wandered around under the tree and occasionally ate an acorn.

I then saw in the distance another deer, coming from where she had come, but this was a buck. I watched him as he came towards where I was. All of a sudden, he walked down into a gully or that's what it looked like to me. In fact what he had done was laid down. I kept my eye on that place where I last saw him and waited. I checked my watch and he lay there for fifteen minutes before he got up and walked on, still coming towards me. My full attention was on him now. When he got to within forty yards of my tree he turned to his left, took a few steps and stopped and peed. This time I wasn't using my bow, I was using my gun. So, I had my gun up and on him the whole time. About six steps later I fired and he dropped and never moved. At that point I wondered what had happened to the doe so I slowly looked around and I noticed she was standing right under the tree I was in and looking towards where the buck was. I guess the shot didn't scare her because there was always a lot of shooting on the marine base.

I have always been curious about animal behavior so I decided to watch her. She kept looking and then took a few steps in the direction of the buck. Then she would stop and stomp her foot. She would take a few more steps, not towards him but back toward the trail where he made his turn. She kept stopping and stomping her foot all the way. When she got to the spot where he had turned, she also turned and walked to where he had peed. Then she paused and smelled, stomped her foot again, then took two steps and saw him on the ground. She jumped straight up in the air and then just stared at him. After a few moments she turned and started back towards the tree I was in and every few steps she would stop and turn her head and look back. After three or four times she was back under the tree stand and did not look back any more, she just kept walking on through the woods. I thought to myself, I will never hunt again after this. I had never witnessed this type of behavior before or since. She seemed to show real emotion when she saw and realized the buck was dead.

Fishing & Friends

I loved to trout fish and most of my trout fishing was with my neighbor Lloyd Younker. Lloyd knew several people that owned land up on the edge of the Blue Ridge Mountains. All the property owners had their land fenced with gates with many locks on each gate. Only the owners had the rights to travel through each other's land. They were lucky because there was a great trout stream located up there. Well, we were lucky too because Lloyd was able to get a key from one of the owners which meant we could go over the mountain whenever we wanted to.

One Friday night we decided to camp up in the area with the goal of going to the trout stream the next day. Keep in mind this area was in the mountains and the roads were nothing but dirt and really rough going. Lloyd had a Jeep but the ruts were so bad if you weren't careful your vehicle would drop down in one right up to the axle. We were careful though and were able to avoid getting stuck. Anyway, this particular Friday night we came around a bend and there was a big black bear crossing the road in front of us. We just stopped and waited as he slowly walked on across into the trees and then stood there and watched us as we went by. Like I said, this place was way up in the mountains.

Anyway, when we got to the top of the mountain there was an open field with nothing but grass and a few small bushes. It was a beautiful place and a perfect place to set up camp so we decided to spend the night there. It was a cloudless night with the stars so bright you felt as if you could reach up and touch them. It was so peaceful. We went ahead and pitched our tent and built a camp fire, eating some of the food we brought with us, and enjoyed just sitting there under the stars. We sat and talked until probably ten o'clock then crawled into our sleeping bags and went to sleep. What a great night it was and especially because I got to share it with such a good friend.

The next morning we got up early, took down our camp site, loaded up the Jeep with all our camping gear and headed down the mountain to where the trout stream was. As we went down this narrow road, there were places where the road slanted so much to one side you could put your hand out and almost touch the ground. We had to use the four wheel drive the whole way and go very slow in order to reach the bottom where the stream was. This stream was called the Mormon's River but it was not a river like you would think. It was actually a small mountain stream with lots of rocks but loaded with Brook Trout. We called them "Brookies." They are beautiful small fish with a great flavor and a real treat to catch and eat. After driving for a while we finally arrived, found a place to set up camp again then headed for the stream.

Lloyd and I would always split up with one of us stopping at one spot while the other would walk on ahead maybe one hundred yards then we would both start fishing. We used fly rods and hand-tied nymphs made to resemble the larvae stage of an insect. Even though we would each go to different places on the stream, we always marked the spot where we started with a broken piece of bush laid on a rock. That way the other person would know to walk ahead and start at another place.

We sure have many fond memories of fishing that stream. One that sticks with me is when on one Saturday morning I went in alone from the bottom down near the lake. I would walk about one mile in to areas that were not fished much, then I would start fishing. This one particular Saturday, I hadn't brought anything with me to eat and I was getting hungry. By this time I had caught two nice Trout so I found a good spot and built a little fire. Brook Trout have no scales just skin so all I needed to do was clean out the inside. After opening the stomach and removing the innards, I cut a green stick and ran it through the fish's mouth and into the end of their stomach. Then all I had to do was put the sticks in the ground on either side of the fire and pretty soon they were sizzling. Sitting there eating those fish on the side of the Mormon's River was so good. It still makes my mouth water. Mmmm.

Another time I remember in particular was when I was in this same area fishing by myself. I saw a big pool of water ahead that was blocked by two large boulders so I went up out of the stream and came up on the side where the pool was. It was a little tricky and the only way I could get to it was between a big boulder and a dead tree that had fallen just past the boulder across the stream. I gathered up my line and pulled it tight keeping my eye on the end of my rod so as not to get it hung on a tree limb. Well, I snuck in real quiet like so I would not spook the fish and had just enough room between the tree and the boulder to get through. Once I got situated, I flipped my line out in the water then lifted the end of my rod and let the fly drift back to me, then I did a "roll cast" by flipping the tip forward again. After several casts and no strikes, I began to back out of the water. I happened to look down and there laying on that fallen tree was a big old snake fast asleep. I had been so quiet coming in I hadn't even disturbed him. Well let me tell you, this time I woke him up good. I yelled so loud and fell backwards so fast I almost broke my rod. I don't know who was more scared, me or the snake, but he went off that log like a bullet and straight into the water. It scared the heck out of me but it's still a great memory of fishing that stream.

Like I said, I did most of my trout fishing with Lloyd but Bill Leggett and I actually fished together too. Yes, that's right. This is the same man who earlier had thought of himself as being above even eating with "the help." However, after working with Bill for a number of years he began to change, at least with me he did. We started to become friends. For example, we both liked trout fishing and on several occasions he asked me to go trout fishing with him. He even asked me to join Trout Unlimited. Being a member of Trout Unlimited meant Bill had permission to go fishing on private property owned by some of the members. I thought about it, then thanked him and decided not to join. Still, I thought it was interesting that he wanted me to become part of a group that he belonged to. As nice as it was that we were becoming friends, I knew Bill still had a certain image of himself he felt he needed to uphold.

Here is one story I think will help illustrate the way Bill thought about himself. One day I mentioned to him that Lloyd and I were going trout fishing and asked if he wanted to go with us. Bill said yes so the next morning he met up with Lloyd and myself, put his gear in the back of Lloyd's old rusted out Jeep, and we all climbed in getting ready to head off. Of course, as a courtesy I got in the back so Bill could sit up front. Well, to get to the stream we had to take a dirt road. Like I said, Lloyd's Jeep was all rusted out so as we went down the dirt road, dust was coming in through holes in the floorboard. I could see Bill was getting a little perturbed and knew he was probably thinking he was a little too good to be sitting in a rusted out old Jeep like this, but I didn't say anything.

Anyway, once we were at the stream, Lloyd and I got our gear out of the Jeep and started putting on our hip-waders. My pair was old and definitely used. In fact, I had used them to pour a patio behind my house and they still had a little concrete smeared here and there. Bill had brought his own hip-waders but he also had a box of new ones with him. As he was trying to decide which ones to wear he looked at me and asked "Is that what you are wearing?" I answered yes, and he then said "I guess these don't make any difference then." My point is, he was always so concerned about what other people might think of him. Even out in the middle of the woods enjoying a day of fishing, maintaining a certain image was something Bill just couldn't let go of.

Still, even though we could enjoy each other's company trout fishing, Bill made it clear he felt it necessary to separate himself from me somewhat. For example, one day he asked me what I was going to do for the weekend and I told him I was going trout fishing. To that he replied, "Well, if you see anyone I know, don't tell them you work for me." He felt that because he was Mr. Leggett of Leggett Stores he had to uphold a certain standard, even down to how he "thought" other people would view someone who worked for him.

I realize I've been talking about fishing but there is more to the situation with Bill I feel is important to elaborate on. It comes up here because some of what I will talk about didn't come to me until I started remembering my fishing adventures with Bill. I guess it's me looking back on situations that I now see with a different perspective. Something maybe I wish I could have done back then. You'll understand more about this later.

Like I said, upholding a certain image was something Bill was very focused on. Raising his kids and having them maintain a certain ideal was also important to him. For example, he was always real strict with his son and daughter. After a while though, you could tell that the boy had rebelled. I would often see him around town in old rumpled clothes, an old leather floppy hat and an unfiltered Camel cigarette hanging from his mouth. Even though Bill had sent his son to many different schools for troubled kids, he never could see what the real problem was.

At the time I could not see it but Bill was slowly getting depressed. Some of the behavioral changes I thought as odd, and maybe even just part of Bill's persona, I realize now were indications of his depression. For example, once when we were walking down the street and someone kind of looked at him, he remarked, "Why is he looking at me?" Nobody was looking at him, but he was becoming somewhat paranoid that other people were sizing him up maybe. As I said, looking back now I can see lots of things that indicated he was going through depression.

It has been said before that depression is "anger turned inside out." For Bill, poor decision making and a short fuse would show itself especially when work was involved. One particular instance happened when we were planning to put a store in a new shopping mall in Charlottesville out on 29 North. This particular area was where all the growth was headed so we felt it was a smart move to put a store there. Our offices would be located there as well. We always bid out our work to different contractors and we did the same for this job. We got a number of bids back and ironically it was Jenné Fixture Company who came in as the low bidder. Remember now, I used to work for Jenné back in Charlotte. Anyway, since Jenné was now located in Georgia we had them checked out and found that he had gone out of business in Charlotte and later opened in Georgia with a much smaller operation.

Bill's opinion was since they were the low bidder, they should do the job. However, I had concerns as to whether Jenné could meet the schedule and told Bill my concerns. Bill's attitude was that they had to follow the specifications, which was true. However, I knew that didn't mean the quality would be there or that Jenné could finish the job on time. Anyway, it wasn't long before we realized that Jenné could not keep the schedule. In fact, when I went down to check on how it was going it was very clear to me that he had to have help. I even talked with Jenné myself, although he didn't remember me. I was not surprised though.

I talked with Bill and suggested we bring some additional people in so we brought in Stanley Fixture Company. They had already done a lot of work for us in the past and were kind enough to send a crew down to help get things done. However, in order to do this, they shipped things to the store without drawers. They were sending fixtures to the store partially completed while we had another crew at the store fitting and installing the drawers. In some cases, even the plastic laminate was applied at the store. We had people working everywhere and it was a nightmare. As a matter of fact, we did not get the job finished until literally the night before opening day, a very good reason for not always going with the lowest bidder. Even with my concerns, Bill had gone forward with a decision that ended up being a big mistake and was yet another indicator that he was not mentally where he ought to be.

Sometime after that we were opening a new store in Dover, Delaware. The day before an opening most of the Leggett's would arrive in town and it was customary for them to walk through the store and check out the way everything was displayed. As I walked with Bill talking about various departments, he noticed one vendor's unit that demonstrated their merchandise. He stopped and looked very carefully at it then called his brother Peter over and began to talk about it. You see, after returning from the armed forces Peter was put in charge of cosmetics and advertising and this vendor's unit was part of the advertising division. Bill felt the unit did not look good enough to be in the store but Peter explained that it was the unit the vendor always used at store openings. Well, first thing you know they were yelling at each other. I stepped in and suggested to Bill that maybe they should talk this out off of the sales floor where all the employees could not hear. However, by this time I think everything had already been said. The point I'm making here is the second generation that Bill came from was very vocal about their opinions and they didn't care who heard. They always thought they were right.

Another one of the family members, Tommy Leggett, was somebody that Bill was always getting into it with. Keep in mind that Bill was all about being very sophisticated, not that Tommy was unsophisticated. It was just that Tommy was, and still is; very comfortable with whom he is as a person. Bill could not stand the down to earth demeanor that was Tommy and when Tommy would walk out of a restaurant with a toothpick in his mouth, it grated on Bill's nerves to no end.

Bill's brother Peter was the same as Bill. I remember one time when Bill wasn't with us we had flown into Charlotte, N.C. in the company plane. Once in Charlotte, we crawled into the Cadillac limousine that the Leggett's kept at the airport for transportation and headed to one of the Belk stores to look at something. Before we got to where we were going we stopped for lunch. Since Tommy was driving, he was the one who decided where we were going to eat. Remember now, Tommy was just a country boy so he stopped at a restaurant called "Po Folks" which was a chain opened by some country singer. We had six people in the car and everyone jumped out and headed for the door. However, I noticed Peter just sat there, so I sat there too. He did not want to go in a place like that, and said so. Had Bill been in the car, he would have reacted the same way. I finally got Peter to go in but just like Bill would have done, Peter complained at how they served our drinks in mason jars.

As we opened new stores the work load became greater and greater so I asked Bill if I could hire someone to help me and he said yes. A fellow from Mississippi by the name of Sam McElroy answered our advertisement. I gave

Sam the responsibility of looking after the existing stores while I took care of all the new ones we were opening. Of course, as I got more involved in the opening of new stores, naturally things would come up at the job having to do with Real Estate. I would always refer them to Bill, but I was getting more and more familiar with that side of our business.

About this time Robert Leggett, Bill's cousin's son, who was a lawyer working at a firm in Richmond, decided to get involved in the business. As a result, Robert asked for, and was offered, a job in Real Estate working with Bill.

Bill's Depression Worsens

Before too much longer, Bill's marriage was falling apart and his wife had left and taken a good part of the furniture. I remember going by his house one day for some reason and it was pitiful the way everything looked. This could not be helping with the way he was feeling but he would not buy anything to make the place look better. An interesting point here is neither Robert Leggett nor I really realized how bad things were getting for Bill. In hindsight, I now can see and am more able to recognize lots of things that I did not see then.

As time went on, Bill became more and more depressed. He had even gone to Vail, Colorado with a friend of his, as he did each year, and when he returned I asked him if he had a good time and he said no he did not. That same afternoon as we were waiting for the elevator, I mentioned to him that they have medication now for depression and he should ask his Doctor about it. At that moment the door opened and he turned and said he had to go to the bathroom. I knew then he did not want to discuss his problem with me and perhaps no one.

His decision making skills had already been less than stellar but I began to notice that he was having problems making decisions pretty much of any kind. I remember going into his office to talk to him one day about something and he was just sitting at his desk with his glasses in his hands, twisting the plastic earpieces back and forth. Even though I had asked him a question, I never got a proper answer from him.

We were opening a new store in a place called Seaford, Delaware and about half way through the developer began having money problems and could not pay the contractors. The developer was building our store and we were going to lease it. So, I reported the problem to Bill and he went to the other Leggett's to decide what to do. At this time they must have felt Bill wasn't up to it, so they asked me to meet with the parties involved and see what we could work out. I did and what we decided to do was we would take over the job, of building our store not the shopping center. We did this because we had made commitments on our end for furniture, fixtures, merchandise and all the other things that go with opening a new store. As it turned out, I began to meet weekly with the contractor who was building our store. I explained to him that we would be paying him, not the developer, because he was now working for Leggett. From that point to completion, I took care of things at the job site and kept Mr. Mason, you remember him, our Controller, informed of our progress. Thankfully, we completed the job on time and opened the store. However, Bill was in no shape to have made the decisions that were necessary to complete that job.

Other Friends

We had two couples in particular that we became very close friends with. We had many good times with Phil Hyde and his wife Kay (a blonde), Bob Romanic and his wife Kay (a redhead) and of course me and Kay (a brunette). We enjoyed each other's company whether it was one-on-one or out at a social event. One particular birthday occasion, we three couples were at the Aberdeen Barn. We had ordered two bottles of Lancers wine, the kind that comes in a stone bottle. When those two bottles were gone, someone ordered two more and this continued until the restaurant said they had run out. We actually drank the restaurant dry of Lancers! No we did not get snookered but we were there until pretty late and had a wonderful time. Bob was a policeman for the city and Phil was a salesman for a company that manufactured electronic parts. We three couples went out a lot and always had fun together. In fact, Phil and I ended up becoming really good friends.

One weekend we, the three Kay's and the guys went to Charles Town, West Virginia to the horse track. On the way up there, I was asked what my lucky number was and I told them the story about seeing the number "5" in the sky when I was a boy and how I always considered five my lucky number. After we arrived at the race track and were seated in the restaurant area looking over the racing form with all the horses, I saw that the fifth horse in the fifth race was named "Nickel Hitter." My friends told me I should bet on that horse so I did, but being conservative I told them I would not bet very much money. Well, wouldn't you know it, my horse won! There were very long odds on him, like 10 or 12 to 1 so there was no way he was expected to win. I still consider five as my lucky number and choose five whenever I can.

Although we three couples did a lot of things together as a group, Phil and I actually became great friends and did a lot of fishing together. I laugh thinking back on some of the things that were Phil. He was a unique sort of fellow, that's for sure. To start with he was a dreamer, always coming up with hair brained get rich quick schemes. For example, he talked about going to Columbia, South America and getting emeralds. He said as a boy he visited his Grandfather there who was an Ambassador to that country. He said he knew how and where to look to find the emeralds. Another wild idea Phil had was stealing the solid gold Angel Moroni from the top of the Mormon Tabernacle near Washington, D.C. He figured we could fly over with a helicopter and cut it loose. Like I said, he was a dreamer.

I guess you could say Phil sort of lived in his own little world and didn't care what others thought or how he should be toward others. For instance, he would show up on a Saturday morning that we had planned to go fishing and wake me up by casting a fishing lure against our bedroom window before I was even out of bed. Another example is when we were fishing and he was running the electric motor, if he broke his line and stopped to fix it, he would be oblivious to the direction the boat was going. We would just sit and go around in slow circles. I wouldn't say anything though. I would just quit fishing and sit quietly until he was ready to go again.

We even bought a fiberglass fishing boat together. When we bought the boat, I told Phil to get a rope so we could tie the boat down on top of the car. Well, when he showed up he had the kind of rope that is used for a clothes line, not the strongest rope in the world and certainly not sturdy enough for what we needed. I told him he should have gotten nylon but we ended up putting the boat on top of the car any way. We turned the boat upside down, tied it down to the car in the front and again in the back and headed for the lake with him driving.

He was zipping off down the road and I was looking out the windshield at the front end of boat wondering if it was going to stay put when suddenly the boat disappeared. Thank God there were no cars behind us because the boat had come off the top of the car breaking both ropes. As it went up in the air it did a complete flip and landed almost flat in the middle of the road, pointing the other way. I say it landed "almost flat" because when we got back to it we noticed there was a hole right at the back and on the left-hand side. We wondered what we could do, I mean, we wanted to go fishing. So I, "being knowledgeable of all things," suggested we take the boat back to Meadowbrook Hardware because I thought I could fix it. So, we tied the boat on carefully and drove slowly back to the hardware store. At the store we bought a new rope and a fiberglass kit, which consisted of a piece of fiberglass cloth and epoxy resin. We put the boat on the ground and I applied the patch and waited for the resin to set up. After waiting a little while we decided that by the time we got to the lake it would be okay, so we took off. When we got to Albemarle Lake, the resin had started to harden so we put the boat in the water carefully and went on fishing. By the time we finished fishing the epoxy patch was hard as a rock.

The next time we were to go fishing I asked Phil, since I was working and we needed an anchor, for him to get an empty plastic bottle and a rope. He said "How is that going to work?" I told him we would fill the bottle with gravel and that would be our anchor. So, when I got home there he was with a bottle of Clorox. I told him, "That won't work," but he said yes it would, and Kay even agreed with him. They figured that since it was heavy it would do the job. It took me a while to explain it to them. Good grief, what I had to put up with.

Like I said, Phil was quite a character. Other things that come to mind is how he would always take these little bottles of beer with him and drink them while he was fishing. When he was finished he would just flip them into the lake. I have always been a stickler for putting my trash in a bag and disposing of it properly, so when he did this one time I backed the boat up, picked up the bottle and told him he shouldn't be doing that. A little while later, after he finished another beer, I noticed him easing the bottle into the water, allowing it fill up. Then he just let it go so it could sink to the bottom. Out of sight out of mind I guess.

Kay, Kay, & Kay

Kay & Phil Hyde

Kay & Bob Romanic

Stopped Smoking

Another bit of information about me is that I started smoking in my early twenties and attempted to quit in my early thirties. This was before I started working for Leggett. I was actually working for Belk in Charlotte when I first tried to quit smoking. What I did was I bought a pipe. I reasoned that I would not inhale a pipe but I was wrong and on top of that I kept dropping tobacco on my drawings. So I switched to those little cigars with the wooden tip but that didn't work either. So, I got serious and finally stopped.

I had not smoked for a month or so when I had to go to South Boston, Virginia with Jerry Kistler. You remember him from my work on Leggett Stores. Well, every time he lit one up he would offer me one (don't ever do that to someone that's trying to quit smoking). Anyway, by the time we made it to South Boston, I had a pack in my shirt pocket.

I continued smoking off and on for several years after we moved to Charlottesville. After Phil and I had the boat I was trying to quit once again and would usually get a cigarette from him. One day before we left to go fishing, he asked me if I had any cigarettes and I said no. To that he replied, "Well, you better get some because you are not getting any from me."

That was just what I needed and from that day forward mentally my mind began to refuse my body of having a cigarette and I got mental pleasure from it. Kind of like if somebody always wanted something from you and you got tired of it, then you started to refuse them and took pleasure from not letting them have it. That's the way it was with me. It gave me mental power over my body and from that day on I never smoked again. It may sound strange but it worked for me.

.

Tragedy

One day while Bill was having a conversation with his brother Gordon, he happened to mention that he had bought a shotgun. This alerted his brother that it was a cry for help because Bill did not hunt and had no use for a gun. Actually, depression ran in their family and Gordon was aware of the signs to look for. With that, the brothers decided to send Bill somewhere for treatment.

He was taken to a place in Greenville, South Carolina as I recall, and was there for a number of weeks. His treatment plan called for him to go home for one week to adjust back into regular life and his brothers had planned to pick him up on a Tuesday. Monday, around noon, Bill asked to go to the exercise area. He had freedom to move around the facilities as long as they knew where he was going to be. About two hours later he had left the property, walked down to Interstate 81 and jumped in front of a tractor trailer truck and killed himself. Another trucker reported later about someone crouching and looking like he was preparing to jump in front of his truck but he had swerved to the other lane in order to miss him.

It is my opinion that Bill felt he just could not go back home and face his friends after being in a mental hospital. You remember, I told you how he was about his position in Charlottesville and how he felt about himself and his family maintaining a certain image. His wife had left him, his daughter was on her own and his son had rebelled against his wishes. How was he going to resume his life now? What would he say to his friends and neighbors? He felt humiliated and decided he would just end it all.

It was that Monday night, near midnight, when the phone rang. I got out of bed wondering who could be calling at that time of the night. I said hello and Robert Leggett, Bill's nephew, said "Sam, Bill killed himself today." I was leaning against the wall and my legs gave way and I just slid down to the floor. I had not considered the possibility of him killing himself at all. I asked what had happened and he told me the whole story.

You see, Kay and I felt we would be there in Charlottesville with Bill for many years to come. In fact, since the girls had all moved out, we had just finished redecorating the whole house. When I heard what had happened to Bill and the initial shock wore off, the next thing on my mind was what was going to happen to our office. Robert said he felt that they, meaning the Management Committee made up of second generation Leggett's, would leave the office in Charlottesville and put him in charge. I said "No Robert, they will move this office," but he didn't think so. I went back to bed and explained the whole thing to Kay. I don't think either of us got any sleep that night.

The funeral was on Thursday in Lynchburg and of course Robert, Sam McElroy, and I were there. On Friday, the Management Committee met and we got the word after lunch that our office would be moved to South Boston, Virginia under the management of Mr. T.C. Leggett (Tommy), who was already in charge of merchandising for the company. The three of us (Robert, McElroy, and me) did not discuss what we were going to do, but by Saturday morning I had weighed all my options and Kay and I headed to South Boston to begin looking for a house.

Moving to South Boston

We did not say anything to anyone but Robert Leggett had already said he wasn't going to move. The next week, McElroy and I were in Roanoke visiting a store and Tommy happened to be there. He came over to us and said, "Come with me, we need to talk." So we went to a private office and he said, "I don't know what your plans are but your jobs are in South Boston." So, on the way back to Charlottesville, McElroy and I talked everything over and decided we were going to move as soon as we could get everything worked out. Robert could do whatever he wanted to.

McElroy was renting a place but I had a house to sell and would also need cash to buy a new house in South Boston. The Leggett Company had store managers moving from store to store all the time but I had heard of some managers taking nearly a year to get their house sold. Thinking more on the situation I was in, I decided to go to South Boston and talk to Tommy. I told him my problem and suggested that if the company bought my house in Charlottesville, then I would have the money for my down payment in South Boston. That way I would not be worried about selling the house back in Charlottesville. He said they had never bought anyone's home before and added it was not their policy to do so, but he didn't say no. So, I went back to Charlottesville determined to work things out.

Back at home I told Kay what had happened and she asked about the value of our house and how much I thought Leggett would pay us for it. We knew we had just finished completely redecorating the house and spent a lot of money in the process. However, we also realized it may not add any actual value to the house. So, how were we going to figure a price? I sat down that night and made a list of everything we had done to the house and the money spent. Then we called a real estate company and had the house appraised. Next, I prepared a long letter to Tommy listing all the things we had

181

done to the house and the cost. I explained to him that when Robert had been hired as Bill's assistant we assumed Robert would be taking Bill's place which meant I could continue my relationship and presence with the Charlottesville office. I felt I would be in Charlottesville until I retired, which was one of the reasons we went ahead with completely redecorating the house. I reminded him that I was fifty years old at this time, the same age as Bill. I explained further how we would have trouble getting what we had in our house when it was sold. I also explained that our three daughters lived in the area, that we had one grandchild, and that we were a very close family. I said anything I thought would help my case. Once the letter was finished, I mailed it to him and waited.

Towards the end of that week I got a call. Tommy told me to go see Mr. Mason. So, I called Mason and we scheduled a meeting for the next day. The morning of the meeting I gathered up all of my information and headed to Lynchburg for my meeting with Mason. When I arrived he was very friendly as he always was. We started our discussion point by point. I explained to him the hardship we were under trying to make all this work and he slowly gave in one by one. I could not believe how well everything was going. At this point I told Mason that I had only one thing left and if we could settle it we had a deal, I told him the last thing and he said okay. I was very pleased and headed back to Charlottesville. You see, when I first approached Tommy he was still not sure what Robert, McElroy or I were going to do. I think this played a part in him agreeing to do what I had asked. I feel that he figured if I came, they would follow.

When I got home and walked in the house, Kay asked how things went and I told her, "You are not going to believe it. We got everything we asked for." Then I explained that the Company would buy our house at the amount we needed to cover the renovations we had done, and I would receive a moving bonus, which was pretty standard in the company. I also called my insurance company, Allstate, and explained to them how Leggett Stores was going to be the owner of the house and they suggested we buy a renter's policy that would cover us until we moved. Things were really starting to come together but things were also starting to get very hectic.

Kay and I went to South Boston and began seriously looking for a house. We quickly narrowed it down to three and when we settled on the one we wanted the negotiations started. The lady of the house was handling everything but wouldn't budge an inch on the price so I decided to see what all I could get her to leave with the house. Finally she agreed to leave the pool table, a chopping block table in the kitchen, a coffee table in the basement and all the window furnishings. At least I got something.

After all the negotiations, the day finally came to finalize the paperwork on the new house. Robert and I were riding together and in South Boston on business so as we were leaving we stopped in Halifax at the lawyer's office so I could sign the papers. I walked in and went over the agreement and noticed the seller wanted me to pay the closing costs. At that point, I had had enough and refused to sign the papers. I went out and got back in the car. I was pissed. When Robert asked what was wrong I told him and he said he would pay the closing costs and to just go back in and settle the thing. I did not agree and said "Let's go home." When I got back to Charlottesville and walked in the house the phone rang and it was the lady seller. She said, "I give up, I will pay the closing costs." We finally had a deal!

Our home in South Boston

After closing on the house we began making plans to move and hired a moving company on the north side of

Richmond to move us to South Boston. Kay decided that all the azaleas she had just recently planted were going with us. The real estate people had already pointed out that some people may not want so much in the yard to take care of so Kay began digging the azaleas and other things up and putting them in pots. We ended up carrying two truckloads of plants down to South Boston and one load was double stacked. When we got to South Boston we put all the plants in the shade and got the seller's son to keep them watered. We were both very happy that we moved the plants to the new house, especially after all the work Kay had done in the yard.

The moving company worked all day packing the truck and it was so full they even had some items strapped to the rear of the truck. They worked past supper time so I went and bought a bunch of sandwiches for them. Finally they pulled out about dark and headed for Richmond to their headquarters. The plan was for them to leave the next morning for South Boston.

As they neared Richmond they took a back road, a shortcut to the north side which was their destination. However, it started to rain and at a curve the driver ran off the road and hit a tree. It hit the tree head on in front of the passenger seat where two people were sitting. The impact caused the windshield to pop out and the two passengers were catapulted out through the windshield but did not get hurt. The impact with the tree caused the truck cab to pivot left, and the momentum whipped the driver down into the vacant seat as a large limb took the top of the truck off. The driver was not hurt. The trailer and its contents were a different story. The impact with the tree split open the top of the trailer and it sat there all night through the rain.

The next morning Kay and I were at the house ready for the truck to arrive, but no truck. I finally made a call and learned what had happened. We immediately crawled in the car with camera in hand and drove to Richmond to the mover's warehouse where they were still bringing things from the accident site. As we began to check things we soon realized everything was broken or damaged. The mattresses were wet and a box of my suits were damaged where the

184

impact had caused the hangers to bruise the shoulders of each sleeve so badly you could scratch it and the fabric would disintegrate. The more we looked, the more we realized it was a total loss. We were devastated. We selected the furniture that we really wanted to keep and contacted a place in Richmond to have those pieces completely restored.

The Insurance Settlement

Once we got back to South Boston it was time to check on our insurance. I called Allstate, the company I had my insurance with in Charlottesville, and told them what had happened. The man I spoke with said the renter's policy only covered us while we were in Charlottesville. I then called the Cincinnati Insurance Company agent in South Boston because I had insured that house when we signed the contract. The person I spoke with there said that if Allstate didn't cover us he felt Cincinnati Insurance would not cover us either. That made me mad and I said to him, "You know I have not met you yet and if you don't want to meet me in court you had better get in touch with your company because somebody is going to cover this thing."

I hung up and immediately called the Virginia Insurance Commissioner in Richmond, Virginia. After explaining everything to him he said that the original policy I had with Allstate in Charlottesville covered me through the move to my new residence, there was no need for a renter's policy. He also told me they had more trouble with Allstate than any other insurance company. Shortly after that I received a call from Cincinnati Insurance Company in Danville where a lady told me she would handle everything and to send all of the paperwork to her. She said they would subrogate the claims with Allstate and the moving company's insurance company and for me not to worry, they had me covered. What a welcomed relief.

I went back to Richmond and took lots of pictures, especially of the antique items we had. I then called our store manager in Winchester, Virginia and asked if he knew an antique dealer that could value the items we had lost. He said he did so I sent him the pictures for the appraiser to review. We did have a few pieces of our furniture delivered to our new home so we would have something to sleep on but that was it. So, that night we spent the night on the floor sleeping on our foam mattress that was stained real bad from getting wet. Other than that all we had was a card table to eat and work off of and three folding chairs we had borrowed. Sitting at that card table we began making an inventory of all our belongings.

Assessing the contents of the house in Charlottesville, we took each room and listed all the items on the floor, tables, chairs etc. and anything sitting on them. Then we did the same thing to each wall. We did this all through the house. This was not that difficult since we had recently redecorated our house. Plus, Kay and I both are very organized and knew what was where in the house. We had to guess at all the things we had in the attic though. With the list complete, we began to place values on each item. We used the appraisers value for the antiques and for the other items Kay went to Green Front Furniture in Farmville, Virginia and they helped to put replacement values on everything else.

With everything cataloged, we submitted the list to the insurance company. It was a twenty-two page very detailed list that included replacement value for each item. I think since we had done all their work for them they accepted it as submitted. Next, the two insurance companies sent someone to meet with us regarding procedures for purchasing new appliances and furniture so we could get our life back together. Both companies agreed we could substitute various things in order to get our home livable.

At this point I went to Tommy Leggett and asked if I could get a bridge loan from the company for $30,000 dollars so that we could begin getting everything for the house. That was not a problem. With that worked out, Kay began the ordeal of buying everything . . . and I mean everything. The things we were able to save and have repaired were the dining room table and chairs, a coffee table given to Kay by her Mother, and two antique chairs we had found in an abandoned house and restored (we called them a "Mr. and Mrs. Chair"). One large antique lamp table made it with no damage as well as a very old wooden tea cart.

Everything else in the way of furniture or appliances was destroyed. We did have one iron bed that made it, scratched but usable but we had quite a few antiques such as corner cabinets, blanket racks, two metal beds, one iron and one brass, (the brass one was bent beyond repair) and many wall pictures that were damaged. Soft items were mostly okay but many things had water damage.

Since we had the bridge loan from Leggett we at least had money with which to purchase replacement items for our new home. Our first submission to the insurance company was about $17,000. The way we approached it was to buy what we needed for the new house and things that suited it. Then we would take our list and check off items that had an equal value to the item purchased, such as a lamp, a table and a chair for a new sofa. Just after we had submitted our third claim, we got a letter back by registered mail stating that things were supposed to be purchased by "like kind and quality" against the lost items and for us not to submit anything else as we had done. It said that we had misinterpreted what the agents had told us. We were just about finished with purchasing things by that time anyway so it didn't matter.

I have to give the credit to Kay for handling all the paperwork in getting it settled. She checked items off as they were paid and stayed on top of everything for as long as it took. Later, after it was all over, if we were out driving somewhere and passed a large moving van, she would begin to cry. It was a lot harder on her than it was on me. I had my work to keep me busy, she didn't. By the time it was all settled it amounted to $42,811.97.

The way Kay and I viewed this whole thing was since we were forced to move, God took care of us in this way. We reasoned that because the furniture we had in Charlottesville did not suit the new house in South Boston, everything was destroyed. Even though that hurt, the final outcome was a new house with furniture that suited the house and that we are still happy with today.

While all this was going on Robert and his wife separated. His wife said she was not moving from her friends in Charlottesville and he said he was not going to live in South Boston. Robert ended up moving to Martinsville, Virginia. He said he moved there because he hoped his wife would come there, but she did not. McElroy bought a house in South Boston on Golf Course Road.

The three of us, Robert, McElroy and me, became part of the Merchandise Headquarters for Leggett Stores. The Leggett store in downtown South Boston had been relocated to Hupps Mill Shopping Center so the Merchandise Division utilized the old Leggett store building space. We moved into a small space on the second floor and proceeded to draw plans for our offices on the first floor. We designed an area for three offices and secretarial space for two as well as a men's and women's bathroom. We had future plans for other offices on this level but the good thing is we finally got back to looking after our jobs full time.

Welcome to South Boston

The manager of the Merchandise Division, Mr. T.C. Leggett (Tommy), had a party at the Country Club to welcome us and our spouses to South Boston. He invited all the people from the Corporate Office and many of the business people in town. He introduced us to the gathered group, telling something about each of us as he went. When he got to me he said this is Sam Lewis and pointing to my almost bald head said, "This is a solar panel for a sex machine." I have never lived that down.

"T.C." as we often referred to him, went to great lengths to help us become a part of South Boston. He first told us that we would join the Country Club, which automatically made you part of the social activities. He also asked Bob Tysinger, who worked for Leggett whom I already knew, to invite me to become part of his hunting group because he knew that was an interest of mine. Bob did and we became very good friends.

Later, I was talking to Kay about the Country Club and I said I was going to take up golf. I did not play tennis and had no interest in going to the swimming pool. So, since I belonged to the Country Club I might as well learn to play golf. Robert and I played together occasionally and he was a little better than I was. One day he bet me $500 I couldn't beat his score with the only stipulation being that it had to be when playing with him. So I took him up on it, I had nothing to lose. That was when I really began to work on my game and I would go and play by myself when I had the time. Almost a year went by and I was getting better and figured I just might be close to winning the bet. Then I started thinking about it more and thought this may not be such a good idea. You see, Robert was my boss so I decided to call the bet off. When I saw Robert, I told him and he gave me all kinds of crap for doing that. It was the right thing to do though because a few weeks later we were playing together and I beat him by two strokes.

Like I said before, Tommy really helped us a great deal in getting involved in the community. But there was a moment when he had doubts about whether our move to South Boston had been the right thing to do. First of all, Tommy was and still is a very religious man and his doubts were based on his religious convictions. You see, right after we moved and the accident happened, Tommy's cousin, Gordon, (Bill's brother) was at the beach. Gordon went out riding his bicycle as he often did but during this particular ride the front wheel came off and he fell. He was banged up pretty bad too. Then that winter, South Boston had one of the heaviest snowfalls they could remember, which prompted Tommy to say to me, "If one more bad thing happens, you're going back to Charlottesville." His comment was because he thought perhaps it wasn't God's plan for us to move and bad things happening may continue. Like I said, he was and still is a very religious man.

Shortly after we moved to South Boston with everything we had gone through, Kay became a little depressed. She did spend a lot of time working in the yard planting all of the various flowers she had brought with her. In the meantime I was very busy with work, getting adjusted to a new work environment along with new people. The thing is that Kay needed something to do and had not found a job yet. This put somewhat of a strain on our relationship. She finally got a job at Boston Lumber Company setting up a decorating department. Although this helped, things were still not where they should be between the two of us.

Well, I was at home one Saturday, sitting in the den with the TV on, while Kay was at work. I wasn't paying any attention to the television because I was thinking about Kay and our relationship. As I sat there I asked God to help us with this problem. As I said that, I heard a voice that came from the kitchen to my right. "You have to do it yourself" is what I heard. It was very clear, to the point that I leaned forward and looked towards the kitchen and said, "What did you say?" thinking that maybe Kay had come home and made the remark after she had heard me ask God for help. It was not the TV because the sound came from the kitchen. This is right up there with the other things that have happened in my life.

Slowly things started to get better as Kay and I both began to get more involved in the community. We had been members of First Presbyterian Church in Charlottesville mainly for the three girls. However, after we moved, even though we visited several churches, we did not join, so our life continued without church. I got involved in hunting and golf and Kay got involved in a number of the local ladies organizations. Over time, we became a part of the community. With all the trials we have been through in our move to South Boston we had settled in, made friends and it had truly become home.

As time passed I got to know Tommy Leggett better. Here are a couple of things I remember. Many times he would walk into my office on Fridays and ask, "What's going on?" so I would begin to tell him what was happening in my job as it related to the stores. Soon I realized that was just an expression of his. He really didn't want to know all of those details I was giving him. However, we would sit and talk about all kinds of things and he would usually end the conversation by asking me what I was doing Saturday afternoon. If I said I was thinking about playing golf, he would say "Get two more and let's play." I was always the one to find two more to play with.

Frequently he would ask me to go with him to visit one of the stores, sometimes we would drive and sometimes we would take the company plane. On one particular occasion, we drove over to Altavista and Tommy took the back road. Along the way he told me about a girlfriend of his early in his life and proceeded to show me where he and his girl friend would stop to make out.

I also remember him telling me that when he first started working for the company, he and his brother Bobby would take the big Cadillac limousine in the winter when the trees were covered with ice and go tree bumping. They would go down through the pasture and pull close to a tree covered with ice and then bump into it and watch the ice fall. Typical kids with big toys.

Follow the Rules

There was a policy that Mr. T.C. Leggett adhered to. One, don't steal from the Company. Two, what happens on the road stays on the road. Three, don't mess around in South Boston. He made it a point to personally tell each one working for him. Then you could not say that you didn't know.

I already knew these rules before I came to South Boston and I told him I knew the rules. He said, "I don't care, I'm going to tell you again so you can't say I did not tell you." When he told me about not messing around in South Boston I got cute and asked "Is it alright to mess around in Lynchburg or Danville?" He snapped back with "You know what I mean!" I knew exactly what he meant. Break one of those rules and you would be fired.

As I mentioned earlier, Peter (Gordon and Bill's younger brother), came into the company after they did and was put in charge of Advertising and Cosmetics. Our cosmetic program was lacking some of the better lines so Peter set out to woo the cosmetic companies into putting their products in our stores and did a good job getting this done. However, somewhere along the way he had fallen victim to the beautiful women that worked in the cosmetic industry in our stores. He was warned and he was warned until the day came that we were opening a store in Suffolk, Virginia. The night before an opening they would always have a dinner for the Leggett executives and some of the upper management people. When this particular dinner was over in Suffolk, the Management Committee had a closed door meeting and Peter was fired. The word spread quickly and T.C. said to some of us the next day, "If we fire one of our own, don't think we won't fire you."

The President of the company rotated among the Management Committee. The Management Committee itself was made up of the four second generation Leggett men. Tommy (T.C.) and his brother Robert, (we all called him Bobby), and their cousins Fred and Gordon. Tommy was now President and so as President he traveled to various stores giving motivational talks to the employees. He had been doing this for a while and had gotten quite good. One day he was going to the Tidewater area for this purpose and Robert and I were traveling with him on the company plane. Somewhere on the way down Tommy started talking about his speech and how good he had become at it and stated he might just go on the lecture circuit. He turned to me and said "Lewis," (he always called me by my last name) "don't you think I would be good at it?" I had always thought he was good at getting up in front of people and talking, so I told him I thought he would, mostly because he had always had a line of bull about him and he had the ability to put people at ease.

Well let me tell you, he looked at me, then turned to Robert and said, "He just told the President of the company he was full of shit." I said "No! No! That's not what I said!" He turned to Robert again and said, "Isn't that what he said?" and Robert said "Yes, that's what he said." Then Tommy said, "You just wait, at the next management meeting I'm going to tell them Lewis told the President of the company he was full of shit." I don't think he did but he was always in good humor.

At store openings on opening morning Tommy would seek me out and we would walk the store on the pretext of looking at the different departments and the décor but what he was really doing was getting information for his talk which he always gave just before we opened the doors. He would ask me questions about a lot of things such as construction problems, things of interest about any of the employees and so on. Many of these things he would work into his talk. His point was to make everyone feel good about the job they had done in getting the store open on time and how good it looked. Without them it would not have happened. He would always finish these talks with this song:

Hey, hey, hey - don't pull that stuff on me,
I'm just a country boy, as plain as I can be.
I ain't so very smart, dumb as any old mule,
Show me a hundred stuck up folks and
I'll show you a hundred foooooollls.

Good Samaritan: One Saturday Kay and I were on our way to Charlottesville to see the children. On the other side of Lynchburg we noticed a lady had pulled too close to the edge of the road and the nose of her car was pointed down into a drop off. We stopped and I took care of the situation by calling a wrecker and got her back on the road.

The next week Tommy received a letter from this lady telling him all about it and thanking him for such nice people they had working for Leggett. Of course, he put it on the bulletin board with "Good Samaritan" written on it.

At Christmas time one year in South Boston we had a contest among the different offices. We were to come up with a Christmas carol and then act it out on stage. The group that I was with decided on "Grandma Got Run Over by a Reindeer" and talked me into being Grandma. Well, I dressed up in one of my wife's skirts and an old shawl. I wore my hunting boots and under my skirt I wore those size 52 red panties. You remember . . . those were the same panties someone put in the shirt box when I worked in Charlotte back in 1968! I hung on to them figuring they would be needed sometime and now was the time. We had reserved the lower level of Ernie's restaurant and when it was our turn to do our thing I was already in the restroom getting into my costume. When the song began I came hobbling out going towards the stage at the other end. I was hunched over like an old person and when I got up on stage and they reached the part about Grandma getting run over by a reindeer one of the secretary's, who was made up to look like Rudolph with antlers and a red nose, ran over and hit me. Of course, I fell down with my legs turned up in the air and my red panties shining. I also had two black hoof prints glued to my forehead and a wig. So every time they would get to the part of the song about Grandma getting run over by a reindeer the young lady would run over and bump into me and I would fall down again. So near the end I pushed my hair back and they could see I had indeed been run over by a reindeer. Well we broke up the place and won first place for the best rendition of a Christmas carol.

My Last Hunting Story

I told you how T.C. had asked Bob Tysinger to get me involved in hunting knowing that was something I liked to do. Bob sure did love to hunt. Now he's retired and still loves it, where I have given it up.

There are two things I would like to tell. The first is when we hunted with a friend of ours, Mark Wenzel down at his farm. He had an old house on the property that we used to hang out in when we were not out in the woods. Bob had been having trouble with a boil or something behind his right ear. It was sore and bothering him. Everyone was sitting around having a few drinks and the subject came up. Bob was saying something about having to go have something done about it.

Well, among the group of us that day were Dr. Les Beach (a surgeon), Dr. Bill McCarty (a bone specialist), and Mark Wenzel (a physical therapist). I think it was Les Beach who spoke up saying, "Hell, we can fix that right here." I want you to know they stretched Bob out on the picnic table that was in the kitchen while one of them went to their vehicle and came back with a black medical bag. They then proceeded to deaden and perform the surgery right there. They lanced it, cleaned it and even sewed him back up.

The next story takes place in North Carolina in 1991 where the same group of us and Phil Rinker, another hunting pal, set up a hunting camp on land owned by William Wilkin's sister. William also hunted with us down at Wenzel's sometimes. Anyway, the old house we were going to use for the hunting camp was in bad shape. The roofs on the porches were falling down and the windows were mostly gone, but we fixed it up nice. We repaired the porches and were able to use the old windows I was taking out of my house as replacements for the missing windows on the hunting cabin.

Bob and I had cut trails all through the property and put up signs such as "I-95," "Boggy Bottom," and so own. We had a map on the wall showing these trails so when we went hunting we could tell everyone this is where we will be. One particular day I had been over to a back field and had seen a lot of deer tracks. Bob and I were discussing this when he told Bill McCarty about it. That's when McCarty said, "You know one deer could have done all that, they have four feet." We just kind of looked at each other.

The next day, which was a Saturday, Bob and I were heading over to one of the Leggett stores nearby where I had had new carpet installed. The manager had told me I could have the old carpet for use in our hunting camp so we left to go get it. On the way we got to talking about what Bill had said to us about the tracks, so I said "I will fix him." So, I proceeded to write this poem about the incident. We mounted it to the chimney in the middle of the living room for all to see. Bill never did comment about it.
It goes like this:

An Ode to Deer Tracks

While walking in the field one day,
I spied some tracks along the way,
I checked them out this way and that.
I showed them to Bob on the map,

Bob got excited and showed them to Bill.
Where upon we lost our thrill,
For Bill exclaimed as a matter of fact,
You know, one deer could have done all that,

We stepped back in disbelief,
As we were told,
Deer have four feet.

Signed The Cat in the Hat*

(*A nickname because I would always sleep in a knit hat)

It Takes Teamwork

While I'm thinking about it I want to share my biggest crisis while working for Leggett Stores. It was not a leaky roof, not a flooded store, not when the developer went bankrupt or remodeling an entire store while we stayed open and doing business. No, it was in Frederick, Maryland when one winter a freak snow storm dumped two feet or more on the store roof. The wind blew it into drifts four feet deep in places. To make matters worse, early the next morning before daylight it began to rain. The snow got saturated with all that water and the roof supports began to sag.

I was in my office and the phone rang. I picked it up and it was the Manager Marc Jordan. He told me about the snow and rain. He said he was concerned because the sprinkler heads were sticking down from the ceiling and some of the rings that fit around them were falling off. He said he had sent some employees up on the roof to see if they could move some of the snow from the deep areas. He asked if I thought the roof might collapse. I said it was certainly possible and advised him to get everyone off the roof and to tell everybody to stay away from that area. I hung up and immediately called our engineers in Charlotte at Belk Headquarters. They gave me the same advice

I called the Manager back and was on the phone when the roof gave way. The area that collapsed was near the Mall entrance where cosmetics started. The roof and ceiling of two column bays were on the floor. Two additional bays were partially collapsed. I left immediately, threw some clothes in a bag and was on the road in thirty minutes. I told my secretary who to call and put the word out to the other corporate offices of what had taken place.

I arrived in the afternoon to police and firemen everywhere and lots of companies wanting to clean up the mess. No one was hurt thank God. The manager and I assessed the damage and talked with several cleanup crews and put them to work in the areas that the firemen and police would allow. There was water everywhere from the snow on the floor and the snow continuing to come in from the roof. All of our carpeting was glued down so it could be saved. We just needed to get the water up and the drying process could begin.

The main thing I had to do was take a complete inventory of the interior damages so that replacement items could be ordered ready for reinstallation as soon as the roof and ceiling were repaired. This was a leased facility so the landlord had to get contractors to make the building repairs. The first thing they did was build a wall around the damaged area. The store had already taken all the merchandise out and salvaged what they could. I had all the fixtures removed, saving what could be reused and dumping the rest. Our security team from Danville came and made arrangements for tight "round the clock" security on the building. I was there for one week then I caught the company plane home, put together more clothes and took the plane back the next day. I was on the job for about four weeks and after that once a week for a couple of months.

Once the roof was back in place things progressed rapidly. Part of the ceiling in the damaged area was sheetrock with alcoves, offsets and curves. The rest was suspended ceiling and that went up quickly. Some of the marble had to be replaced where it had been scratched or broken. After all the repairs were completed, the new showcases and other items came in. I spent most of my time on the sales floor with the plans directing where everything belonged. All the various company divisions had people there ready to offer help wherever they could. Many of our other stores sent people also. We had the same teamwork that we had when opening a new store. The great thing about Leggett Stores was how each group worked as a team doing their thing, so the store would always arrive at completion and always on schedule.

Have I told you how much I loved my job? I knew what was expected of me. I did it and everybody left me alone. **I loved my job**.

Downsizing & Selling the Company

In other areas of this book I have told you about people, places and events concerning my job and the people I worked with. Now in order to explain to you the downsizing and selling of the company I will have to touch on some of these again. What I will disclose is from my perspective and various bits of information I was able to hear personally or was told.

The Leggett Company had corporate offices in Lynchburg, Danville, and South Boston. Each office was headed by one of the second generation sons, Gordon Leggett in Lynchburg; Fred Leggett in Danville and T. C. Leggett in South Boston.

In the late 1960's W. E. Leggett (Bill) one of Mr. Harold Leggett's four sons went to Charlottesville, Virginia as Manager of the Leggett store at Barracks Road Shopping Center before taking over Real Estate and Store Development.

Third generation Robert Leggett son of R. A. Leggett (Bobby) of Henderson, N. C. was educated as a lawyer in Richmond, Virginia. He had worked briefly in an Attorney's office before coming to work for Bill Leggett In Charlottesville, Virginia.

In 1970, I moved to Charlottesville from Charlotte, North Carolina to assist Bill in the Store Planning area. Later Bill began to look for someone to help him in Real Estate. He interviewed several people and finally settled on Robert Leggett who wanted to come to work with the company and this was his chance. Robert was married and had one child. His wife did not want him to take the job because she liked the Richmond area and did not want to move. He took the job anyway. Robert moved to Charlottesville around 1983 and several months later his wife came but their marriage was in trouble. My first encounter with Robert was cordial but careful. On several occasions he asked me questions or suggested things that I felt were not proper. I felt he may have been testing me. Robert and I worked together on several projects as we were opening many new stores at that time.

Around 1985, Bill's marriage fell apart and he became depressed. The running of the office in early 1986 was left up to Robert and me along with Sam McElroy who had come in to help me a few years earlier. We were actually in the middle of having a store built in Seaford, Delaware and things were a mess. The developer was in financial trouble and not paying his contractors so work on the shopping center, as well as our store, was lagging. I spent a lot of time at the job. We began to pay the subcontractors in order to complete our store, knowing we would get our money back from our lease payments to the developer. Robert was very supportive of the suggestions and decisions that had to be made to keep the job progressing.

In June of 1986, Bill killed himself. Robert thought the office would be turned over to him. That did not happen. We were told to move to South Boston. Robert moved to Martinsville with the hopes that his wife would follow. She did not. Eventually, he did move to South Boston and bought a house. Time passed and Robert and I worked well together. He handled Real Estate and Leases and did a very good job. Of course, being a lawyer really helped. He was a very good negotiator and I had great respect for his abilities.

Around 1992, Robert convinced T.C. Leggett to let him go to Lynchburg and work with Mr. M.E. Mason, the company's financial controller. T.C. agreed, partly I think so his oldest son Tom could take over Real Estate. When the time came to make the move, Robert wanted to take the store leases and continue to handle the Real Estate end of the business. His reasoning was he would not have enough to do in the beginning and handling Real Estate would keep him busy. I asked him why he wanted to go to Lynchburg and into finance and control. He said, "Cause that's where the power is." He went to Lynchburg and I stayed. T.C.'s son Tom did not take over our area. My early impression of Robert in Lynchburg was Mr. Mason and his assistant, Mr. Stinnett, shared little with him. Robert had an office on the first floor and they were on the second.

In 1994, the following is what I think took place. In the three or four years Robert had been in Lynchburg, he had conversations with Mason about the profitability of the company. Mason approaching retirement suggested or implied that the company should be downsized or sold. This idea over time began to grow. Peter, who had been fired in 1987, was brought into the discussions and he agreed.

I don't think there was any connection but about this same time my salary was frozen.

In July of 1995, a meeting was held by Robert, Mason, Peter, Gordon, and their brother Reid, who was a New York stock broker. The purpose of the meeting was to discuss how to go about selling the company. Everyone was told "to keep their mouth shut." I know this because of what Peter said in February of 1996. The first step was to downsize the company to make it more profitable because the more profitable the company, the more it is worth. To do this they wanted to get rid of the Management Committee and install a CEO. This would make one person accountable thereby streamlining the decision making process
The Lynchburg faction wanted Robert in the controlling position in order to facilitate their plans. However, there was opposition. T.C., Fred and perhaps the Belk's wanted Fred to be CEO. A deal was finally struck that Fred would be CEO and Robert President. Robert and the Lynchburg faction went along not wanting to give away their real intention which was "to sell the company." Downsizing began. The Lynchburg offices were moved to Danville.

Back in February of 1995 I had a meeting with Robert and he told me my office would be moved to Danville. Sam McElroy, my assistant, would be transferred to the Charlotte office in Store Planning. Robert told me to begin shifting what I was doing back to the Charlotte office and to make plans to reduce my hours to four days a week in six months. I think he had to do that to me so the downsizing worked across the whole company. I say this because Robert was thinking that in six months, plus or minus, the company would be announced for sale. With everything that was going on, what I was doing began to dry up. The store managers, nervous about the changes taking place, stopped calling. Soon I had nothing to do except some remodeling in a couple of stores. I mentioned to Robert one day that I had very little to do and he remarked, "Keep quiet and stay out of the way." I did and began work on a book that was a compilation of years of family poems, notes, and sentimental writings.

In the meantime a push is on to get a new man to run the Merchandise division in keeping with the new profitability plan. Sandy Mosby had been asked to retire from that position. The sellers go along with the idea. In October of 1995, a new man is hired to take Sandy's place.

In late February 1996 an announcement was made that an offer had been made to buy the company. A committee was selected to look into it. The committee is made up of Robert, Mason and Reid. At this time, Peter made the comment, "They told us eight months ago to keep our mouths shut." That coincides with the **July 1995** meeting when the sale of the company by the Lynchburg faction had seriously been discussed.

March 26, 1996, meetings began to take place with prospective buyers. I was asked to get photos of a typical Leggett store.

March 27, 1996, Robert and Reid are now working on a severance package.

In late March, 1996, Fred Leggett, realizing what had been going on without his knowledge, resigns as CEO and Robert was voted in to take his place.

April 15, 1996, Piedmont Mall with controlling interest by Belk was taken out of the proposal.

May 15, 1996, a meeting in Richmond was held with a prospective buyer.

June 3, 1996, all leases were copied.

June 13, 1996, another meeting was held in Richmond.

June 17, 1996, T.C. Leggett was voted off of the Board.

June 20, 1996, Robert asked me to get plans of seven stores for use at a Board meeting.

July 10, 1996, another meeting was held in Richmond to clarify a buyer's offer.

July 15, 1996, a meeting was held in Richmond to clarify the Belk offer.

Finally the deal was done! Belk bought Leggett Stores which was the best fit since Belk owned 20% in the company anyway.

Belk sent Dave Stovall, Jr. to run the company. I knew Dave, Jr. because his father had been manager of several of our stores. Dave, Jr. wanted to move the offices to Richmond for better recognition as a company. I knew because when the company was bought, Belk did not buy the Real Estate. Many of our stores were owned by Leggett Reality Company which included the office complex in South Boston. The bulk of the now Belk Corporate Offices were in that building. The lease was about up and Robert was threatening to not renew the lease, trying to force Belk into purchasing all the Real Estate. Because of that Dave, Jr. had me trying to find temporary space to move into if a deal could not be struck. This never occurred because they were able to get a lease extension. Perhaps Belk agreed to buy the Real Estate at a future date, I don't know. A couple of years later Belk did buy all the Real Estate causing T.C. to remark, "We ain't poor no more."

When I first found out that Dave, Jr. planned to move the offices to Richmond I decided I was not going so I announced my retirement. It was a tough decision. I was only 60 years old. Kay was working though so I was able to get on her health insurance plan. I also talked with my investment guy and he said he thought I would be okay.

Dave came and asked me to stay, because we had two remodeling projects underway. I thought about it and suggested to him that I would complete those jobs on a consulting basis which meant I would be able to come and go as needed with the use of my office. I would submit my charges on a monthly basis at the agreed upon rate. That way I would not have to get involved in all the other things he wanted to do. I continued to work with Belk and completed the two projects, which took about a year. He did end up moving the offices to Richmond. Anyway, I retired and took up the leisure life. It wasn't all that smooth though. I had two years before I could get Social Security and five years before I could get Medicare.

After one year Kay could not stand it and wanted to retire also but if she did we would have to buy our own health insurance. She did end up retiring and I was stressed out over the cost of insurance, her spending money, my spending money, you name it. Suddenly, I was depressed so bad I didn't even enjoy going to play golf, and then I lost my appetite. I spent one month sitting in my chair in the den while taking antidepressants and finally came out of it. Once Social Security started and Medicare kicked in things got a lot better. We did experience a significant financial setback in 2008 when the economy hit bottom. We still have not fully recovered from that. So, even though the circumstances of how I retired were not what we had planned, Kay and I have been very happy and are really enjoying retirement.

Last Days with Mom and Dad

I loved my Mom and Dad very much and made it a point just before they died to tell them what good parents they were. They seemed to appreciate that message before they died. In 1989, Dad was in the hospital very sick so I came down from Virginia to see him and ended up staying with him that night in the hospital. I talked to him about our lives and how he had raised us and the accomplishments of each of us. We had all done very well. Nobody had gotten into any real trouble, even though one did spend a night in jail.

We had been taught from a very early age to work hard and that no one gave you anything. Whatever you got, you had to work for. None of my brothers and sisters, nor I, have had more than a high school education. In fact, my brother Mendel and I are the only ones who finished high school. However, we all have done well in our life pursuits.

I remember sitting on the floor at my Mother's feet the week before she died in 2002 and telling her what a good Mom she had been. I talked to her for a long time. She had trouble talking because of a stroke but her responses were "I've been a good Momma," "I've been a good Momma." I'd like to think my acknowledging that she was a good Mom gave her peace of mind before she died. I think we all have that on our mind as death nears. We question what kind of person we have been during our life and it is reassuring to hear someone certify that you were a good person.

Kay and I were at Montreat, North Carolina for a church conference when my Mom died. My friend Jack Brown was with me when I got the word. Kay and I had taken extra clothes prepared for the news and left that day for South Carolina. She is buried next to my Father in Rock Hill, South Carolina. For those of you who have someone who has had a stroke or has Alzheimers, but especially people that have had strokes, talk to them even though they can't respond because most, if not all, can understand what you are saying. Include them as much as possible.

Months before Mom died, I was visiting with her and my sister who was caring for her. I was talking with my sister while my Mother sat there with us. If someone can't respond to us we tend to not talk to them. After my sister got up to do something Mom looked at me and said, "Talk - To – Me," pointing to herself. That is why I sat at her feet the week before she died and gave her my complete attention. Be kind to old people, we may be old outside but inside we are still in our twenties.

First Presbyterian Church

Kay and I had thought about going back and getting involved in church again, but even after a few years of being retired we still hadn't settled down and picked one out. It wasn't until after Kay's father died that we really started to look for a church. You see, after the funeral service in Rock Hill, the church where Kay's sister Debra attended invited the entire family over for a meal at their church. We noticed how much they showed compassion and concern for Debra's family, and how comforted she was at having them as part of her life. So, when we got back home to South Boston, Kay and I talked about it and decided it was time for us to seriously look for a church to join.

After visiting several churches, we settled on First Presbyterian Church in South Boston. Kay liked it for the interior colors and the comforting feeling it evoked and I liked the Pastor, Russell Lee. Russell is a South Carolina fellow and I liked his approach to things. However, Kay and I didn't join right away because we wanted to be sure this was where we wanted to stay. One Sunday, a business meeting was being held after church and all church members were supposed to stay for the meeting. I was getting ready to leave but Kay wanted to stay. We ended up leaving that day but I told her on the way home how I thought that since we were beginning to feel like part of the congregation at First Presbyterian Church, we should join. We did join and have been very happy with our decision. While we are very active in the church in our own way, we tend to shy away from any politics and the relationship between us and the church has been great.

Like I said, Pastor Russell Lee grew up in South Carolina and I really liked his style. Although he was the Preacher of the church we attended, he and I also became involved in activities outside of the church. For example, after attending First Presbyterian Church for a while, Russell found out I used to build boats and asked if I would help him build a Scull. A Scull is a very long and slim type of boat and the same kind you see college kids racing. Well, I didn't think a Scull for Russell was such a great idea. I figured he would turn over and drown so I suggested a version more like a canoe. He agreed so I drew up plans and we got started building it.

I had started building a work shop in the attic space above our carport but at the time Russell and I started building the boat, the only access to that work area was by using the pull-down attic stairs and walking through the attic area to the space above the carport. I hadn't put a door going to the outside yet, but the shop did have a front window. As far as the boat was concerned, the plans were to build it and then take it out the front window.

Russell and I ended up working on the boat for several months. The finishing touch was the wooden eagle's head I hand carved and then mounted on the front bow of "Miss Liberty" (a name Russell chose). When we were finished, and just like we planned, we took "Miss Liberty" out through the front window and to the lake for her maiden voyage. It was a warm day in November when the launching took place. Russell really put her through her paces but with every test, she handled very well. We were both very proud of our accomplishment. In fact, the construction of the boat, bringing "Miss Liberty" out of the window and even the launching had all been featured in the local newspaper. Since that time, Russell and I have used my shop to make several items including an oak desk for his office.

I began to carve many walking sticks, with Russell trying his hand at it too. Although I have a passion for fine detail and intricate carving, Russell's approach to woodworking is more rustic. I have always been very precise about the construction and finish of what I build and I had always wanted to try wood carving by hand. So, I began to work at making walking sticks and carving different decorative features on them. On some, I carved faces and on others the walking stick itself was carved to look like a snake.

Each walking stick was numbered and identified with a stone or a sea shell that I collected and polished myself. The stones I collected from a number of different places but the sea shells I found in Nags Head, North Carolina. I also made it a point to make a walking stick for each of my three daughters and even made a hand-carved African drum for my oldest daughter, complete with a deer-hide drumhead and a hand carved "Drummer Girl" on the front. In addition to the walking sticks, I have made many canes for the older folks at our church that need some help getting around.

African drum I made

While coming up with ideas for different things that Russell and I could work on together, he and I decided to try our hand at making wooden toys. The design of the toys fit nicely with my precision style of woodworking but worked equally well with Russell's more rustic creative approach. We would work every Monday on designing and building different toys and would always end the day having he and his wife Marilyn over for dinner. In Christmas of 2013, we gave away about thirty-five various wooden toys that included ducks, dragons, horse and wagons, cars and even tractor trailer trucks. All of the toys had moving parts so they were a lot of fun for the kids as well as the adults.

Around 2010, after the economic downturn, I told Russell that I may have to go back to work. He asked doing what and I told him I thought I would start making small tables. They would need to be small because my shop was also small. He told one of the church members what I was planning to do and since this member was building a new house, he asked me to build some tables for him, which I did. Since then, I have been building many tables of varying designs. Two in particular have wooden flower inlays worked into the design of the table. More recently I have built Patrick Henry corner chairs and am now trying my hand at Cremation Urns. Between my wood shop and playing golf, I have a lot to do and stay quite busy. Kay is very busy with her activities as well. She is involved in numerous clubs and organizations in the community, plus she does oil painting.

As you can see, through our fellowship with First Presbyterian Church, we have made many friends. It has enabled us to have a "family" outside of our regular family and one we feel very comfortable and at home with. We are really happy with our decision and can't imagine ever leaving.

Below is a cute story that a good friend of mine from the church, Diane Newberry, requested that I include in this book. The people mentioned in the story are all friends that are part of our church family. Enjoy.

"The Great Panty Caper"

It was February of 2005, and here in South Boston Virginia, a real good friend by the name of Diane Newberry had a birthday party at someone's house. Part of the birthday fun was to trash Diane's yard. So, while everyone else was at the party my minister, of all people, and I did a thing called "forking" the yard. You do this by sticking plastic forks in the ground all over the yard. Of course, we had to take it a step further by adding little Whirly Birds that blew in the wind. We also hung a happy birthday sign on a line between two columns on the front porch and put an old commode with the lid down and toilet paper on a stick near the road.

The other thing we added was those size 52 red panties. You remember, the ones from 1968 given to me as a gag gift? They were the same ones I wore at the Christmas party as Grandma in the skit "Grandma Got Run Over by a Reindeer." Those panties had been around for a long time!

I had been hanging on to them knowing they would come in handy one day. This was the perfect time so we hung the panties on the line between the columns of the front porch underneath the happy birthday sign. After we finished "forking" and decorating the yard, we headed back over to the party.

When the party was over and we all went back by the house to see the reaction to what we had done to the yard we noticed that the commode lid was up and there was toilet paper scattered across the ground. No one said anything about it at the time so we had Diane sit down on the commode and pictures were taken while we laughed and carried on about how funny it all was. Diane and her husband Barney went to bed that night and figured they could take some more pictures the next morning before cleaning up the yard.

Well, at 11:30 that night Carol and Mark Foster, who had to leave the birthday party early, went by to see what we had done to Diane's yard. They said at that time the panties were still hanging between the columns. However, the next morning when Diane and Barney went out to take pictures and clean up the yard the panties were gone! It was then that they noticed someone had actually "used" the commode. We figured this and the kidnapping of the red panties must have happened while we were all at the party but we didn't know.

Anyway, the point is that the size 52 red panties that had been a gag gift to me in 1968, and served a fun purpose during a Christmas carol skit while I was with Leggett, got one more laugh shared among friends. Alas, after thirty-eight years they are now gone but they served us well in the three major events surrounding these large red panties. So ends the saga of "The Great Panty Caper."

My Friend Jack Brown

Jack and I met when we began going to First Presbyterian Church and immediately became great friends. He was always inviting me to go play golf with him and some of his friends and we always had great fun. However, he did not necessarily take the game seriously. At times he would have fireworks in his bag and when you least expected it one would go off, sometimes on your back swing. He also did not always follow the rules. One time, I was playing with him and two other fellows we had invited, Lewis Chappell and Clyde Hall. While we may not have taken our game very seriously, Clyde sure did. Anyway, Clyde was riding in the golf cart with me and on one hole, Jack and Lewis "pulled their drives left" (meaning they shot the ball way to the left) and Clyde said, "I think they are out of bounds." I looked at him and said, "They won't be by the time we get there." Sure enough, after hitting our balls and heading back over to them, they were "miraculously" in bounds. While it wasn't exactly "legal" it was all in good fun.

Jack's two favorite words were free and cheap. I even nicknamed him "Freche." He nicknamed me "The Big Man" and while I'm not sure exactly why he gave me that nickname it may have been because I was better at golf than he was. Anyway, one day on the golf course we were teeing off over a lake and when I hit my shot it didn't quite make it and ended up in the water. That's when I heard him say in a sarcastic tone, "The Big Man done hit it in the water." One time for his birthday I got him a golf hat with the words embroidered on the front, "I beat The Big Man." When I gave it to him I told him he wasn't allowed to wear it until he beat me. Well, one day he did beat me and made me put our scores on the hat and sign and date it, "78 to 79, October 20, 2007." He gave the hat back to me before he died. I keep it hanging on the wall to remind me of the great times we had.

Jack also enjoyed giving me a hard time about the Mazda sports car that I drove. I always picked Jack up and take him home in the Mazda. He was always fussing about me driving "that little car." So I decided that I would do something to fix Jack about teasing me. At church we had a men's group that met every Thursday night. Some of us would meet at a restaurant and have supper before the meeting. I told this group to meet early at the restaurant next time. The next week when we met to eat, I had a limo waiting. We all piled in and went to pick up Jack. When he walked out you should have seen his face. After that he never said anything else about my "little car."

Most of the time, when we got back to his house, we would sit out front and talk about life and the hereafter. One time we were talking and I said to him, "Why don't we make an agreement to come back after our death if there is any way." He agreed and our friendship rolled on.

Then Jack got sick and one day we were joking about who might be going first. So I reminded him about our agreement. He said yes he remembered and we would do that. He continued to have more problems. Finally he was told there was nothing more they could do, his heart was failing. Jack accepted his situation completely. One night when I was visiting him I mentioned that it looked like he would be going before me and was he still good with our agreement. He said he was.

I went by to see him frequently and one day when I drove up he was sitting on the porch smoking a cigarette. I got on him about his smoking and he said, "It can't hurt me now." As time passed, he continued to get worse. His wife called one day and asked if I could come over and shave him. He was not able to get out of bed to do it himself and would not let her do it. So, I went over and shaved him. When I was finished I bent over and asked him if he remembered our agreement. He nodded his head yes. Then I told him when it came time to go don't fight it, just let it go. He nodded his head again and I said my last goodbye and left. When I got in my car I broke down and cried like a baby. The next morning about seven thirty he died. That was a sad day for me.

That night I went to bed thinking about Jack and finally went to sleep. Around three thirty in the morning, I was asleep when suddenly something bumped my bed hard. I woke up with a start and the first thing I said was, "Jack is that you?" At that moment, I felt someone sit down on the foot of the bed opposite from where I was laying. It startled me so I reached for the light and turned to see what was there, but there was nothing. I lay there and moved my feet and did everything I could to replicate what I felt and could not. The bumping of the bed was exactly the kind of thing Jack would do. I think Jack visited me that night. What do you think?

A couple of weeks before he died a friend had visited him and Jack had asked if he knew where he could borrow a box to put his ashes in for the church service. Well, when I heard this I went over and told him not to worry I would make him a box. I began to make one for him, however he passed away quicker than I expected so I had to hurry to get it completed in time for the service. It was truly a labor of love.

Jack was always telling a joke and enjoyed jokes as well. We all enjoyed his humor. I think he would have had a laugh the evening at the funeral home when I put his ashes in the box, handed it to his son and commented, "We finally have Jack in the box." I miss him very much and at communion I have two pieces of bread. One is for Jack.

Rest in peace Jack

Summary

I hope you have enjoyed reading about my life and the times I grew up in. If I have repeated myself please forgive me, some memories just keep coming back. I will be seventy eight in September of this year, 2014.

When you are older you too can look back and see events and patterns in your life and realize God really is in control. So, God bless each of you. I hope your life can be as full as mine has been.

Kay and I in our retirement years 2014

Family Pictures

Family picture around 1940 Shulerville, S. C
Back Row Left to Right: Dad, Mom, a cousin and Lester.
Front Row Left to Right: Furman, me, Alma, Evie. (Mendel
is not in the picture, either he was an infant
or had not been born yet).

My Family 1965 Rock Hill, S. C.
Left to Right: Mendel, Evie, Me, Mom, Furman, Alma, Lester

2002 – My brothers & sisters
Standing Left to Right: Mendel, Alma, Evie, me, Lester.
Furman is seated. Family reunion at Alma's lake house near
Lancaster, S.C.

Rock Hill, S. C. 1962
Kay and I at Kay's sister's wedding

Later Years
Children & Grandchildren

Three Daughters - Jeanne, Sammie Kay, LaDonna

Jeanne's son Rodes

LaDonna's son Cody

Left: Jeanne's daughter Riley
Right: LaDonna's daughter Kristen

Our family Christmas 2013
Three daughters and four grandchildren